AGILE PROJECT MANAGEMENT

How to Skillfully Implement Scrum, Run Effective Teams, and Cultivate High-Performance Leadership

TOM HILL

of the Publisher is provided beforehand. Any additional rights reserved.

Furthermore, the information that can be found within the pages described forthwith shall be considered both accurate and truthful when it comes to the recounting of facts. As such, any use, correct or incorrect, of the provided information will render the Publisher free of responsibility as to the actions taken outside of their direct purview. Regardless, there are zero scenarios where the original author or the Publisher can be deemed liable in any fashion for any damages or hardships that may result from any of the information discussed herein.

Additionally, the information in the following pages is intended only for informational purposes and should thus be thought of as universal.

As befitting its nature, it is presented without assurance regarding its prolonged validity or interim quality. Trademarks that are mentioned are done without written consent and can in no way be considered an endorsement from the trademark holder.

TABLE OF CONTENTS

INTRODUCTION

Welcome to "Agile Project Management: An Agile Introduction to Scrum Mastery. Learn How to Implement Core Value, Best Practices, and Essential Mindset in Agile Leadership". Thank you for taking the time to read this book. If you are brand-new to Agile, then you will find a great deal of information that will help you get on the right path in the world of Agile.

If you are a seasoned vet in the world of Scrum and Agile, then you will surely find a fresh perspective on some of the most common discussions in the world of project management. As such, you can expect to find a new and updated twist on many of the classic issues surrounding this important topic.

The world of project management is quite large. There is a large number of project types and approaches which can be implemented in order to carry out a project. But one thing remains constant regardless of the type of project or approach which you use: the need for results.

The fact of the matter is that customers, end-users, and project sponsors all want to see results. It doesn't matter how or who delivers. The main point is to get the job done. And, while that is fair, the truth is that it puts a great deal of pressure on project teams to deliver.

In the world of traditional project management, many project leaders find themselves stretched thin because they need to deliver a high-quality outcome at a reasonable rate. The days in which project overran in terms of cost and budget are long gone. These are the days of efficiency and getting the job done with as little resources as humanly possible.

However, there is an important caveat: this doesn't mean that you are going to cut corners. In fact, those projects which resort to cutting corners and short-changing customers end up become a lot more expensive in the long run. When quality is sacrificed for the sake of time and effort, the project deliverables end up being of inferior quality. In the best of cases, this can grind away at the project team's reputation. In the worst cases, it can leave a project team on the hook for the changes and modifications that may have to be done after the fact.

This is where Agile plays a key role in ensuring that projects get done right, straight from the beginning. Now, most folks believe that Agile itself is a project management methodology that holds any number of secrets, tips, and tricks. The fact is that Agile is a mindset. What this means is that since Agile is a mindset, the practitioner needs to believe in what they are doing firmly. If an Agile practitioner is not sold on the effectiveness that Agile can provide their efforts, then it might be best to simply seek another philosophy that is more in line with the practitioner's beliefs.

Throughout this book, we will be defining what an Agile mindset really is, what it entails, and how it can be used to enhance project performance. What this means is that your newfound mindset will enable you to find the best and most effective way to lead your team down the right path.

What this means is that if you believe that Agile is a cookie-cutter approach that can simply be overlaid onto any type of project, then you are mistaken. Agile is a living entity that evolves along with the project team. Of course, there is a number of rules, guidelines, and recommendations which need to be considered while implementing Agile. Ultimately, the project team will end up tailoring the Agile mindset to suit their own strengths and abilities.

Also, we will be taking a look at Scrum as the most common and proven Agile project management methodology know to date. Truth be told, Agile has consistently delivered on its billing time and again. While it does have its nuances, it is not nearly as hard to put into practice and other more complex project management methodologies. In fact, it is quite easy to implement once the core principles and ideas have been taken into consideration. What this means is that any, and all, Scrum practitioners need to first adopt the Agile mindset before jumping in headfirst into Scrum.

Think about it along with these terms: you need to put the horse before the cart.

What does that mean?

It means that you cannot reasonably expect yourself or your team to effectively carry out Scrum as a project management methodology without actually being sold on its effectiveness and the benefits which it offers project management professionals. But before you can be sold on Scrum, you need to understand the main difference between traditional project management methodologies and Scrum. In addition, you need to be convinced that Agile, most notably Scrum, can help you boost your overall performance and the quality of your output.

Consequently, this book is for both seasoned project management professionals as well as novice professionals who are looking to dive into this world. Perhaps you have had a cursory introduction into the world of Agile but still haven't extracted the essence of it. That is why this book has been designed to help you get the core of Agile and then build on that into the implementation of Scrum.

What this means is that you won't have to go through large and complex guides that often read like the instruction manual for your refrigerator. The fact is that this book has been developed in a light and the crisp manner in which you can get the most information out of it without having sifted through esoteric language claiming that Scrum is the end all and be all of project management.

In reality, this book backs up its claims through years of experience in the implementation of Scrum. Sure, there are theoretical aspects to Scrum, but the fact is that the majority of the claims and ideas presented herein are the result of experience, both good and bad.

So, let's jump right into the meat and potatoes of this book. We are sure that you will find it both useful and informative. Buckle up because this is going to be one exciting ride.

Chapter 1

INTRODUCTION TO THE
AGILE MINDSET

In the introduction, we emphasized the importance of the Agile mindset. As such, we are going to drill down in this chapter about what the Agile mindset is and how it pertains to Scrum, and any other Agile project management methodology for that matter.

At its very core, the Agile mindset is all about embracing change. While traditional project management methodologies are all about predictability and reducing project uncertainty to tables, charts, and algorithms, Agile is not only not afraid of uncertainty, but actually used uncertainty as fuel to drive the project forward.

However, this doesn't mean that Agile projects are run off the cuff, so to speak. Agile projects are run in such a way that they factor in uncertainty as part of the standard operating procedure. What this means is that all Agile practitioners are clear on the fact that things can take a 180-degree turn at any time. While it is highly discouraged to make significant changes on the fly, Agile and Scrum practitioners are essentially ready for anything that might come along.

With that mind, the Agile mindset is more about a shift in philosophy in which uncertainty is most welcome and even encouraged up to a certain point.

This can be a bit of a stretch for some folks.

In traditional project management methodologies, the focus is on creating a sustainable environment based on predictability. Of course, there is nothing wrong with having this approach. If anything, predictability is useful, especially when looking to get things done right, right from the start. However, there are cases in which uncertainty comes to the forefront of affairs.

That being said, are traditional project management methodologies outdated?

Not necessarily.

Nor are we saying that Scrum is better than a traditional approach. The fact is that it all boils down to the particular set of circumstances under which a project is being conducted. Therefore, having a keen understanding of those conditions will make it easier to implement the right methodology for the project at hand.

Traditional project management methodologies are very good for those projects which deal with established practices and principles. In such cases, there really isn't much guesswork going into the project. If anything, it is a straight shot. The project leadership is experienced, and they know what they are getting into. The terms of the outcomes have been clearly established. So, there isn't anything to negotiate once the project has gotten underway.

A great example of an ideal project for a traditional methodology is road construction. Road construction is one of the project areas that don't make significant shifts in a short period of time. In fact, civil engineering is one area that has perfected many of its methods.

As such, this means that engineers don't really have to guess much when it comes to building a road. Unless a project is looking to build a road in an area where there is no road at all, or some new technique is being pioneered, there is very little room for chance.

In this example, project leadership can be confident that there isn't going to be much change involved. So, the project team can confidently have at it. Given the fact that the amount of uncertainty has been clearly accounted for, the degree of confidence in the project's outcomes should increase significantly.

However, traditional project management methodologies proved to be rather inadequate in environments in which uncertainty is a constant rather than an outlier. In such cases, it can be rather difficult for a project team to gain a strong foothold. Therefore, project teams need to adjust on the fly so that they can address changes as they come.

This is business as usual in the software industry. When developers set out to produce new software, they often run into uncharted territory. While they may be experts in coding and building programs and applications, they may not be quite so adept in the specific field they are working on. What that means is that the results of the software being produced are unpredictable, given the fact that it has never been done before.

Can you see the difference between building roads and building software?

Truthfully, building roads, no matter how many times it's been done, still carries a certain degree of risk involved. Nevertheless, experience and best practices help project engineers mitigate the risk involved in road construction.

In the case of software engineers, they may not necessarily account for the entire scope of risk involved in a project. Mainly, the influence of customers' demands throughout the project places a greater amount of pressure on the project team to deliver the features customers expect.

Now, you might be thinking, why does change occur so frequently in software development?

The fact is that change is constant in any field that often produces uncertain outcomes.

Think of marketing. Any time there is a new product launch, the results of the marketing for this new product are highly unpredictable. Even the best of products can flop if its marketing is not done properly.

However, marketers can't accurately predict the outcome as the human factor accounts for a large percentage of the product's success.

What this means is that anytime there is a high degree of the human involved, the more unpredictable the outcome will be. In short, whenever people are involved, the chances of something unexpected happening are greater. Sure, there is the possibility of some fortunate accident leading to welcome results. But the likelihood of getting lucky with uncertainty that is rather slim.

With the boom of the software industry in the 1980s, software developers began questioning the effectiveness of traditional project management methodologies available to them. They were looking for a set of guidelines that could provide them with the flexibility they needed while ensuring the full range of operational capabilities needed to address the challenges that generally arose during software development practices.

Several attempts throughout the 1990s led to some emerging Agile methodologies such as Kanban (which was a system developed by Toyota in the 1970s) and Extreme Programming (XP). XP was perhaps the first solid attempt at creating a full-scale Agile methodology that could encompass all of the aspects that pertained to Agile project management. One of the most relevant contributions of XP was the understanding that it is possible to produce more, in less time, while taking change into consideration.

The main point of divergence between traditional project management and Agile is that Agile projects are broken down into phases. Each of these phases must yield some type of output that is susceptible to testing, thereby allowing the customer and stakeholders to see the direction the project is headed. In this manner, the project team can receive feedback at various points in the project while incorporating change at designated points of the project.

In the traditional project management realm, a change could only be accounted for once the final product was ready for inspection. This meant that the project team needed to put the entire product together and then test it before it could be subject to change.

In doing so, project teams have little to no feedback throughout the lifecycle of the project. Needless to say, this can lead to some surprises at the end of the project's lifecycle. Most importantly, if the customer, or any other stakeholder, request changes to make, some of these changes may not be able to get done. What this means is that an important feature might have gotten left out because of a lack of timely intervention.

Consequently, the need for a set of clear guidelines that could enable project teams to work under the Agile mindset led to the creation of the Agile Manifesto by the 12 original developers of the Agile methodology. These individuals were software development professionals who had plenty of experience under their belt within the domain of Agile project management methodologies, except they hadn't realized that that was the direction in which they were heading.

So, after some brainstorming and collaboration, the following manifesto emerged as a declaration of a new project management approach that would encompass all of the elements which had become vital to the software development field.

> *We are uncovering better ways of developing*
> *software by doing it and helping others do it.*
> *Through this work, we have come to value:*
> *Individuals and interactions over processes and tools*
> *Working software over comprehensive documentation*
> *Customer collaboration over contract negotiation*
> *Responding to change over following a plan*
> *That is, while there is value in the items on*
> *the right, we value the items on the left more.*

In this manifesto, it is important to note the flexible and dynamic orientation of this mindset. The phrase "we are uncovering better ways of developing software by doing it and helping others do it" is a call to action for constant change.

This call for change is a stark contrast to the traditional approach in which sustainability through predictability is the hallmarks of successful project management. This is also a clear declaration of how change and uncertainty are paramount to the successful development of skills, and not procedures.

That last point is, perhaps, one of the most telling signs of how Agile is not your typical, run-of-the-mill cookie-cutter, solution. Agile is all about finding a better way of doing things all the time, and then showing others how to do it.

That being said, the four main components of the Agile Manifesto make a clear case for the need to shift focus in a more outward direction, rather than establishing procedures and rules with regard to how things ought to be done.

First, "individuals and interactions over processes and tools" underscores the need to focus on developing personal skills and abilities over fool-proof processes. Traditional approaches espouse the creation of procedures that are carved in stone. So, rather than striving for developing excellence in people, traditional approaches strive for the creation of excellent processes. In a roundabout way, the traditional approach value processes over people.

Second, the statement "working software over comprehensive documentation" is another clear difference between Agile and traditional methodologies. However, this statement is also subject to criticism from Agile's detractors. Notably, detractors claim that Agile advocates for a loosey-goosey approach. This, in turn, leads to a lack of formality in the way processes ought to be carried. In short, there is a claim that Agile is more about improvisation rather than setting clear targets and goals.

To that claim, it is important to note that Agile values time as the most precious resource at the disposal of the project team. As such, Agile values getting work done more than drafting professional manuals. After all, documentation can always be developed as a part of the project. But any time documentation takes precedence over getting things done, time is being poorly used.

Third, "customer collaboration over contract negotiation" is another clear indicator that Agile project management is all about fomenting collaboration and working as a team rather than drawing out contract talks with lawyers and other advisors. While this doesn't mean that there are no contracts involved, it does mean that there is a clear focus on getting stuff done rather than going over the fine print. There is always time for lawyers to do that.

Finally, "responding to change over following a plan" does not mean that things are done in a haphazard manner. What it means is that Agile practitioners are more concerned about rolling with the punches rather than following guidelines that are set in stone. This also entails that whenever there is a bump in the road, this bump should not derail plans. If anything, bumps, and even detours, are nothing more than a part of the usual course of business. At the end of the day, if there is a need to alter course, then so be it. The main focus is to get around obstacles as quickly as possible.

While this philosophy permeated the software development landscape, more comprehensive approaches sought to systematize Agile into rules and guidelines, which could lead to a robust framework. These frameworks were not intended to become standard operating procedures, but rather, the rules of the game in which the players had freedom of movement.

Initially, this led to methodologies, such as the Dynamic Systems Development Method (DSDM), Lean Management, and Crystal. Also, Six Sigma also joined the party due to its comprehensive data-driven analysis methodology. The incorporation of Six Sigma into the

Agile world led to the creation of Lean Six Sigma. This is a project management approach that is highly sought after by manufacturers who are in the constant need for improving efficiency at every turn.

However, the most mature and fully operation Agile project management methodology is Scrum.

The name "Scrum" comes from the term used in Rugby. If you are familiar with this sport, Rugby teams must work together in order to keep the play moving. While it is similar to American Football, the main difference between Rugby and Football is that Football has continuous stoppages in play. Rugby, on the other hand, doesn't have nearly as many stoppages. Therefore, athletes must keep the ball moving until one team scores a point. Nevertheless, teammates must work together to protect the teammate who has the ball. When a player sees that they are about to be caught by the opposing players, they must get rid of the ball and pass it to another teammate in order to keep the play going.

This is why the term was borrowed from Rugby and put to use in Scrum. As a result, Scrum is a highly collaborative approach that values teamwork over individuality. While individual talents are highly appreciated, an individual will never be more than the sum of all parts put together.

Given the fact that Agile, and later Scrum, were born out of the software industry, there is a widespread perception that Agile is applicable to software development only. However, this could not be farther from the truth. In fact, Agile is applicable to any industry and field of work because it is a mindset and not a set of rules. Of course, Scrum has a clear set of guidelines. But it is important to note that they are guidelines and not a flowchart.

As you will see throughout the rest of this book, Scrum is all about using these guidelines to direct the natural flow of an industry or manufacturing process. When you are able to implement Scrum effectively, you will begin to see new ways of improving processes, thereby saving time and resources. Most importantly, effective Scrum practitioners see people for what they are and not as interchangeable parts that complement a machine.

Please bear in mind that nothing is perfect. Consequently, Scrum is far from perfect. But for now, Scrum is the most flexible and lean approach which has been developed in the project management field. While we are not advocating that it is superior to any other type of approach or methodology, the benefits it provides to its practitioners have been widely proven. So, do take the time to read on and find out how Agile and Scrum can help you become a better project manager.

Chapter 2

FUNDAMENTALS OF A SCRUM PROJECT

After having gone over the foundations of Agile, and a brief history to boot, we are now going to jump into the fundamentals of a Scrum project. So, this chapter will focus on the overall process, that is, how a project can go from its conception all the way to its completion. The main thing to keep in mind is that this is an overview and that subsequent chapters will delve deeper into each one of these areas.

A Scrum, just like any other project, begins with a need to get something done. It is a common misconception to think that a project itself is permanent. In fact, a project is a temporary action that leads to a permanent outcome.

Think about it is along these lines: a project is called to build a project. So, the construction of the bridge itself is temporary. It will last, however long it takes to build it. The bridge itself is permanent, as it will hopefully last for a very long time.

If the project were permanent, then the construction of the bridge would go on forever with no clear outcome in sight. Consequently, the stakeholders in the project would never see the deliverable come to fruition.

This is why projects respond to specific needs. Someone, somewhere, has decided that they need to get something done. Whatever it is, there is a desired outcome that must be achieved. In the end, there is a tangible outcome, which is the result of the endeavor set forth.

In the case of manufacturing, there is an ongoing process that is carried out with the aim of having regular production of an item or the delivery of a service. In this case, the process is continuous and is permanent. The outcome is also permanent as it results in the delivery of goods and services to customers.

In either situation, Scrum can come into the mix and provide leaders with the tools they need to keep the chains moving. Of course, the main difference is the way in which the process is conducted. As such, project leaders (notice that we don't use the term 'project manager') are in charge of making sure that the process goes according to expectations.

One of the most common misconceptions about Scrum is that it is very light on planning. The fact that Scrum does not advocate for voluminous documentation does not mean there is no planning involved. The main difference is that the planning that is involved is done in such a way that all team members have input, and visual instruments are used to relay the planning conducted at the outset of the project and at the beginning of each sprint.

Typically, most Scrum projects begin with a project sponsor. The project sponsor is someone who believes in the need for developing a certain product and will back its creation within the organization. Furthermore, a project sponsor may be adamant about the use of Scrum as the preferred project management methodology.

The project sponsor must now get to task on assembling the necessary components for the project.

The first thing that a project sponsor needs to sort out is the Product Owner. The Product Owner is the person who will spearhead the project itself. Now, it should be noted that the Product Owner is roughly equivalent to the project manager though it is worth mentioning that Scrum has a flat structure. Therefore, the Product Owner is not really the "manager." The role of the Product Owner is known as the "voice of the customer." Thus, the Product Owner acts as a liaison between the project team and the customer. This takes away from any potential attrition, which may derive from the back and forth interaction between the team and the customer. By having a centralized point of contact, the customer has someone they know they can talk to while the team focuses on doing their job.

Typically, the project sponsor and the Product Owner will come together to find the Scrum Master. In some cases, it will be the sole responsibility of the Product Owner to find a suitable Scrum Master. Other times, the project sponsor may want to have a say in that decision. However, the customer must not intervene during this process. Ultimately, the customer has no say in which members make up the team.

The Scrum Master is essentially a facilitator. This role involves making sure the project team has everything they need in order to carry out the tasks. Also, the

Scrum Master does not have any functional authority over the project team. The Scrum Master role is essentially a coordination role between the team and the Product Owner.

Then, there is the project team. The team generally consists of 4 to 6 members. Each member is officially designated a "developer," though they may not necessarily be developing anything in the sense that software development considers it. As such, these members are the ones who are in charge of getting the job done. They don't "take orders" as they are left to self-regulate their workload. What this means is that the project team is free to determine what they will do in each sprint and who will do what.

Once the team is assembled, the project can get underway. However, there are some administrative steps that need to happen before the project can officially get off the ground.

Firstly, the Product Owner is in charge of drafting the Project Charter. The Project Charter is a document that establishes the terms and conditions of what will be done throughout the project. This includes all the details pertaining to the deliverables, the time that the project will last, the number of members making up the team, the duration of sprints, the responsibilities of all the parties involved, and any other specifications such as change requests and the scope of the project itself. All of these elements need to be established in writing so that the team doesn't go on an endless quest trying to add more and more features that were never discussed at the outset of the project.

Once the Project Charter has been agreed on, the Product Owner must also make sure that financial terms are also disclosed. This is important when a project team is working with external clients who hire the project team for a task. If this is the case, then the Product Owner may seek legal counsel in drafting a formal contract that will stipulate the terms of the Project Charter but is legally binding terms.

The project officially begins when the terms of the Project Charter have been agreed upon. The Product Owner can then go about assembling their team and get everyone on board. This leads to the very first meeting known as the Project Planning Meeting. In this meeting, the entire team convenes to discuss what is expected of them, responsibilities, and the scope of the project.

From the Project Planning Meeting, the creation of User Stories is born. User Stories are the fictional depictions of who the real end-users of the final deliverables will be. It is common to give them a name and a face so that the project team knows who they are developing the product for.

Once user stories have been defined, the project team can then move on to the first Sprint Planning Meeting. In the Sprint Planning Meeting, the team will decide how much will get done in the first sprint. This amount of work is entered into the Sprint Backlog. The Sprint Backlog is the collection of tasks that will be done in that block of time.

However, there is a general Product Backlog in which the entire workflow of the project has been laid out. From this generalized Product Backlog, the Development Team (Scrum Master plus developers minus the Product Owner) will decide what elements will be included in the sprint backlog. This is what needs to be done in the time allotted for it.

At the end of a sprint, the Sprint Review Meeting takes place. This is the time when the customer can get a glimpse of what is being developed. It should be noted that the customer needs to see something right from the beginning of the project. Even if it is in embryonic form, the customer needs to see their vision come to fruition in some manner.

After the Sprint Review Meeting, the Sprint Retrospect Meeting is conducted by the entire project team so that they can go over the good and the bad of the previous sprint in order to fine-tune performance. It should also be noted that this is the appropriate time to go over any change requests.

This is the Scrum process in a nutshell. It should be noted that what differs Scrum from other project management methodologies is its iterative nature. That means that the process can be repeated as many times as needed in order to get the job done. As such, each iteration is a sprint. The project will have as many sprints as it needs to get the job done. Of course, it should be noted that the project team needs to make a realistic assessment of the number of sprints that are actually needed so that they can avoid taking up more time than needed.

In the next chapter, we will get into the details of how a sprint is actually conducted.

Chapter 3

THE SPRINT OF A SCRUM PROJECT

The meat and potatoes of a Scrum project is the sprint. Scrum's nature indicates that it is an iterative methodology meaning that its process is repeated over and over. What this entails is that the Development Team must get into a groove early on so that each subsequent sprint happens without a hitch. That is why we are going to be taking a closer look at how a sprint ought to be conducted.

Typically, a sprint lasts for about four weeks. While this figure isn't set in stone, it's usually the best amount of time because it not only coincides with a calendar month, but it is also a round number that is easily manageable. You will quickly notice that Scrum deals in even numbers due to their divisibility. While there is nothing wrong with odd numbers, they are simply harder to divide when making plans.

Now, the first step in each sprint is the Sprint Planning Meeting. This meeting takes place right before the beginning of each sprint. It can happen the day before the sprint gets underway. Also, it can happen over the weekend so that the team gets off the ground on a Monday morning. Perhaps the project will officially begin on the first of the month, and that happens to fall on a Thursday. So, the team meets on Wednesday to conduct the Sprint Planning Meeting.

In this meeting, the Sprint Backlog is created. This is the list of tasks that will be conducted by the Development

Team. The Sprint Backlog can take any configuration that suits the team. Ultimately, the configuration must be one that leads to an outcome that can be seen by the customer and/or project stakeholder.

In some cases, the Sprint Backlog can be a collection of individual tasks that are needed for the project at that stage, or it can be one, a large task that is composed of numerous smaller tasks, that when put together, build the larger task.

It is also important to note that the Product Backlog is the reflection of the User Stories created by the Product Owner (or entire project team) at the outset of the project. As such, the Sprint Backlog needs to reflect the individual User Stories being addressed in a particular sprint.

Furthermore, a User Story cannot be officially considered as "finished" until all of the functionalities pertaining to that user have been developed. For example, if a mobile application offers to deliver any number of features for a given type of user, the User Story will be finished until that particular user get all of the features that the application offers to deliver.

In addition, there is nothing that obligates the Development Team to complete one User Story per Sprint. In fact, a User Story might be so large that multiple sprints are needed in order to produce all of the functionalities. By the same token, multiple User Stories may be completed throughout the course of a single sprint. The fact of the matter is that the team must decide what they can realistically achieve with the time they have been allotted for that given sprint.

At the end of the day, it doesn't matter what the team chooses to do. What matters is that the Sprint Backlog be logical and realistic. The main point is to maintain a sustainable pace. Scrum advocates a sustainable pace so that the Development Team doesn't burn out midway through the project. Scrum does not call for 12, 14, or even 16-hour workdays. If the team is comfortable with an 8-hour workday, that is fine. If the team is comfortable with a 10-hour day, then so be it. But anything that calls for marathon sessions is not conducive to a sustainable pace.

A word of caution: if the customer is running out of time and the team is asked to work on a short deadline, it is better to reduce the scope of the project as opposed to asking the team to work longer hours. Ultimately, the team and the final deliverables may end up suffering for it.

Once the workflow and responsibilities have been dished out, the Development Team can get to work. Please keep in mind that Scrum calls for self-regulating teams. This means that neither the Product Owner nor the Scrum Master has the authority to assign, delegate, or otherwise order, what needs to be done. The team must come up with a reasonable arrangement that plays off the individual talents of every member. This leads to a harmonious environment in which everyone feels like they are in control of their own work.

At the beginning of each workday, the Development Team meets for the Daily Standup Meeting. The Daily Standup Meeting is a short interaction, typically lasting no more than 15 minutes, in which the Development Team debriefs on the previous day's work and looks ahead to the day at hand. This is the appropriate time to bring up any issues or obstacles that may have been encountered. For instance, if a computer suddenly stopped working, the Scrum Master needs to figure out a replacement computer, fixing the broken one, or getting additional help. Whatever the issue, the developers must bring it up with the Scrum Master, who, in turn, may escalate the issue with the Product Owner. This escalation is not due to authority, but rather, it is due to practical purposes. If there is a need to purchase another computer, then the Product Owner may need to make arrangements to procure the requested items.

It should also be noted that the Daily Standup Meeting receives its name because the team is not invited to sit and drink coffee. This is a short meeting in which the team needs to be brief and go over relevant items only. After all, it is better to focus for a short period of time than to waste valuable time on topics that may not be relevant to the project.

As the team goes through the sprint, the Sprint Backlog must be groomed by the Scrum Master. This means that all tasks which are completed need to be taken off the board. This helps the developers focus on what needs to be done. It is also a psychological device that helps the team see the progress they are making. In addition, it is the Scrum Master's ultimate responsibility to deal with administrative issues such as keeping track of the tasks which are done and what needs to be done.

One important thing here: if, for some reason, the Development Team falls behind schedule, the Development Team can make a decision on the ground. They can accept that they have fallen down, leave tasks unfinished and pass them onto the next sprint, or drill down and get them even if it means staying late for a few days.

This particular decision is a matter of the Development Team. The Scrum Master may suggest their preferred course of action. However, it is the entire team that decides how they want to approach the situation. Whatever the final course of action is, the team must keep in mind that they should not overextend themselves. Otherwise, they may run out of gas at some point before the project is completed.

Once the Development Team accomplishes the goals set out during the Sprint Planning Meeting, the team will be ready to hold the Sprint Review Meeting. In this meeting, the Product Owner will join the Development Team, along with the customer (or project sponsor) to see the progress made by the Development Team.

As such, the demonstrations which are conducted are intended for the stakeholders to see where the project is headed and what the deliverables look like up to that point. It is very important that testing is conducted prior to the Sprint Review Meeting. When deliverables are presented without being tested, unexpected glitches may pop up. This may prompt the customer to provide feedback or request changes that may not have otherwise come up.

Once the customer has gotten a glimpse of the deliverables, the customer, stakeholders, and other interested parties will meet with the Product Owner to provide their feedback. This feedback will be collected by the Product Owner (without the presence of the Development Team) and then transformed into a series of lessons learned that the Development Team can take into account for the following sprint.

The feedback session is called the Sprint Retrospect Meeting. This is the entire project team going over customer feedback as well as their own impressions of the last sprint. Feedback and change requests will then be included in the Product Backlog and address when appropriate.

The Sprint Retrospect Meeting officially closes the sprint. The next sprint then begins with another Sprint Planning Meeting in which the project team charts out their course for the upcoming sprint. Hence, this is the manner in which Scrum is iterative as opposed to other types of methodologies out there.

Chapter 4

ROLES AND RESPONSIBILITIES IN SCRUM

Thus far, we have mentioned the players that make up a Scrum project team. However, we are yet to discuss who these players are in greater detail. That is why we will use this chapter to focus on the specific roles in Scrum and what the breadth of their responsibilities is.

But before we dive into the description of each role, it is worth reiterating one key point: Scrum has a flat structure. What this means is that there is no hierarchy within the project team. Every member stands on equal footing and has an equal say in the decisions that are made. The difference of each role depends on what the functions of that role are. However, the responsibility and authority are the same.

What this means is that anyone can assume a leadership role within the project. In fact, it is encouraged that all members take the point at various times throughout the course of the project. This largely depends on the individual expertise of each member. So, if some members are uniquely qualified to take the point in a certain area, then, by all means, they should.

That being said, let's being with the Product Owner. As stated earlier, the Product Owner is the "voice of  the customer." What this means is that the Product Owner acts as a buffer between the Development Team and the customer. What this does it that it avoids unnecessary wear and tear on the team. Since the team does not have to deal with administrative details, they are free to focus on the task at hand.

As such, the Product Owner will liaise between both sides. Also, the Product Owner should be the most experienced Scrum practitioner as they may be called in to provide guidance on how Scrum processes should be conducted. Again, this does not mean that the Product Owner has "authority" over the team. It simply means that the Product Owner has more experience and is ready to use it in order to guide the team in the proper course of action.

Generally speaking, the Product Owner is the first person to come on board for the project. Consequently, it is the Product Owner's responsibility to draft the Project Charter, find the Scrum Master, and put the User Stories together.

As far as the assembly of the Development Team goes, this can be done in tandem with the Scrum Master. As far as the User Stories are concerned, the Product Owner can draft them up alone, or use their Development Team's expertise to come up with the individual stories. However, the Product Owner must not delegate this task to the team. The Product Owner must be involved because they are responsible for transmitting this vision to the customer. As a result, the Product Owner must be involved in the creation of the User Stories.

The second role in Scrum is the Scrum Master. The reason for calling it "second" is because most Scrum projects start off with a Product Owner who then brings the Scrum Master on board. There are times when a project sponsor may have the perfect Scrum Master but needs someone to fill the Product Owner role. In this case, the Scrum Master might come on board before the Product Owner.

Nevertheless, the Scrum Master's main role is to facilitate the day to day activities of the Development

Team. This entails doing everything that is required for the team to get the job done, but not actually doing any of the work. While the Scrum Master may help out in a pinch, it is not the Scrum Master's responsibility to do any of the work. In fact, the Scrum Master may know very little about the actual work being conducted so long as they are keenly aware of Scrum methodology.

While it is not advisable to have a Scrum Master who lacks knowledge in the technical work being done, it is certainly no impediment if the Scrum Master does not have much experience in the technical area. For instance, if the project calls for building a skyscraper, the Scrum Master does not need to be an architect. Of course, it would help if they were, but so long as the Scrum Master is adept in Scrum methodology, they can lead the team in the project. After all, it's the team that does put the actual project together.

The Scrum Master's role is defined as "servant leadership." So, this means that the Scrum Master is at the service of their team but must also take the point when needed. This is especially true when the team runs into an obstacle. While other team members might be adept at dealing with the issue, the ultimate responsibility of dealing with the problem should fall onto the Scrum Master's shoulders.

As such, it is the Scrum Master's role to alleviate pressure from the Development Team so that they may be as efficient and focused as possible. Indeed, the Scrum Master plays a dual role of leader and support.

Next, the heart and soul of the Development Team is the individual developer. Scrum utilizes the term "developer" to refer to the team members who actually go about the crafting of the final deliverable. Therefore, the developers are in charge of making sure that the Sprint Backlog gets done. While the Scrum Master is in charge of grooming the Sprint Backlog, it is the developers who must take ownership of the individual tasks that need to be completed.

The profile for a developer needs to be in line with the project that is to be conducted. However, knowledge of Scrum methodology is not a prerequisite. So, a developer might join the team with little to no experience in Scrum. This is why the Scrum Master and the Product Owner must be seasoned vets in the ways of Scrum. Their expertise will guide the developers in the manner in which the tasks must be completed. However, the actual work is up to the developers themselves.

By this logic, the develop has freedom of action. This means that the developer can carry out the tasks as they see fit. The main thing to keep in mind is that the final outcomes must be in line with what the customer has asked for. Beyond that, the developer has very little responsibility.

One other important aspect that falls within the scope of a developer's role is testing. In the specific case of software, testing is a crucial part of ensuring that the project deliverables meet the expectations of the customer and relevant stakeholders. Consequently, time needs to be set aside for testing throughout each sprint. This will enable the team to make sure that what they have produced will be up to par with the client's requests.

Up to this point, we have defined the various roles in a Scrum team. On the whole, a team would be comprised of roughly 4 to 6 developers plus the Scrum Master and the Product Owner. So, a Scrum team could range from about six to 10 members overall.

Earlier, we made the point that Scrum likes to deal with even numbers. This is especially relevant to the developers. The main reason for this is that the developers can be paired up when needed. Naturally, this would not be possible with odd-numbered teams.

Furthermore, teams smaller than four members, while certainly functional, may run into trouble at some point. By the same token, teams greater than six developers may prove to be too large. In an upcoming chapter, we will address the issue of having large Development Teams or even multiple teams.

However, there is still one more player to be heard from: the Agile coach. This player is not commonly introduced into Scrum teams since an Agile coach is not a formal part of a Scrum team. The Agile coach is a type of technical support. This is a renowned expert in the area of Agile methodologies. The role of the Agile coach is to guide the Scrum team, especially when the organization is brand-new to Agile, or if there are significant discrepancies in which the Scrum methodology is being implemented.

Consequently, an Agile coach is an impartial third party who will provide their independent perspective on the way the Scrum methodology ought to be put into practice. In some cases, an Agile coach may accompany the entire Scrum team throughout a project while they find their bearing. Once the entire team is comfortable in the ways of Scrum, the Agile coach may sit back and offer pearls of wisdom whenever needed.

One other way in which an Agile coach may intervene in by being available on an "on-call" basis. What this means is that if the team has questions or is unsure about how to handle a particular situation, they will call on the Agile coach to provide their tutelage as needed.

On the whole, Scrum teams are tight-knit teams that deliver high-octane results. The best Scrum teams are the ones that have been working together for a while. As such, the more a team works together, the better and more adept they will become.

Chapter 5

ARTIFACTS IN SCRUM

After having taken a good, long look at what a Scrum team is like, we will now drill down into one of the most important aspects of effective Scrum project management: artifacts.

Artifacts in Scrum are essentially the ways in which Scrum practitioners can measure the degree of effectiveness a project is yielding. While success can be seen in the achievement of the project outcomes, the fact is that Scrum has a very clear concept of success. This measure of success is seen in staying on track with the way activities and tasks have been planned out. If the Development Team is able to stay on course within the allotted time, then the project is highly successful. However, if the Development Team veers off the mark, then it is necessary to figure out what happened and why it happened.

As such, each of the artifacts in Scrum has a specific purpose. When put together, they make up the project's dashboard. As such, the team is able to gauge their performance and make any necessary adjustments.

The first item on the list of artifacts is the Product Vision.

In short, the Product Vision is the overall objective the team has to achieve for the project. This is the overarching goal that needs to be accomplished in order for high-fives to go around at the end of the project.

A great example of a Product Vision could be developing an application for a banking institution. Another example could be constructing a building, or better yet, a working prototype of a new device or machine.

In all of these examples, there is an outcome that needs to be met.

The Product Vision is essentially what the customer or project sponsor wants to achieve. However, outsiders may have a very rough idea of what they are looking for. They may not be aware of the functionalities and features which could be incorporated into the final product. Moreover, they may not be aware of how realistic their expectations may be.

So, it is up to the Product Owner to give the customer a ballpark regarding what they can expect to achieve, given the time constraints and financial limitations they might be up against. If a customer's expectations are completely unrealistic, multiple projects may be negotiated in order to lead up to the customer's final vision. On the other hand, if a customer is aiming too low, the Product Owner may provide them with a more robust alternative.

The Product Vision can be summed up in a simple, one-line statement. Something like, "our customers will be able to conduct their transactions through our application from the comfort of their smartphone" may very well encompass the spirit of the project.

The Product Vision is then translated into Scrum language through the User Stories. The User Story, or Stories, will give the Development Team something to aim at. After all, "a banking application" is a rather vague concept. This is why User Stories are so important when it comes to providing the Development Team with the guidance they need to create the final solution.

Consequently, the next artifact is the User Story. A User Story is essentially the actual user of the final deliverable. If we are talking about a car, then the User Story must answer the question: "who will drive the car?" In fact, it is amazing how often companies get this wrong. They create a product with one type of customer in mind, yet a completely different market segment ends up making the product a success. User Stories need to be as elaborate as possible. This will give the developers a clear goal to shoot for.

A User Story for a new car model could look something like this:

Ben, 30, is a marketing professional. He is single and a college graduate. He lives in an upscale section of a large, metropolitan area. He lives in a two-bedroom apartment on a high floor of an upper-class condominium. Since he lives within walking distance of his office, he doesn't drive to work every day. He likes to go out into nature on the weekends to do some fishing or hike up in the mountains. He is very active on social media. His social life is also very important to him.

In this example, we have given a name to the fictional end-user of the vehicle being designed. It is also a good idea to create an image of this end-user. In this manner, the Development Team can have a clear idea of who they are building the car for.

It should also be noted that some projects may have multiple users. Therefore, multiple User Stories must be crafted in order to address every one of the potential end-users. This largely depends on the type of product and the range of features and/or models the project may contain.

For example, the vehicle being designed may have several styles and trims to suit the specific needs of the various types of customers the company is shooting for. However, there might be a case in which a product such as a smartphone may have to contain a host of features in order to have a broader appeal.

From the Product Vision and User Stories, the Product Backlog is formed. The Product Backlog has one overarching goal (the Product Vision), which is then broken down into smaller chunks. Each chunk may represent the outcome of individual sprints or may simply be the logical manner in which the workload can be divided.

The member in charge of grooming the Product Backlog is the Product Owner. They are in charge of making sure that the larger tasks are being fulfilled. Also, since the Product Owner is the liaison with the customer, the Product Owner must be able to give answers to the customer when status updates are requested.

There is no fixed number of items or tasks that the Product Backlog must contain. The Product Backlog simply needs to have the number of items relevant to the project itself, and that's it. Please keep in mind that attempting to standardize Scrum procedures may lead to obstacles down the road. So, if one project contained five items, there is no reason to believe that the next project should have the same amount. In fact, one project may have five items, while another may have a hundred! It all depends on the nature of the project.

When the Scrum team sets out to run its first sprint, the Sprint Backlog is created. The Sprint Backlog is the list of items that will be completed in an individual sprint. Now, it is important to note that the tasks and activities that will be conducted as part of the Product Backlog and the subsequent Sprint Backlog need to synch with the User Stories for the project. In essence, any activity that does not contribute to developing the functionalities outlined in the User Stories is simply a waste of resources.

The Development Team defines the Sprint Backlog. The developers, in conjunction with the Scrum Master, must define what they can reasonably get done within the timeframe afforded to them. So, if a sprint is set to last four weeks, then the Development Team needs to figure out what they can do in that time.

This point is crucial when setting up the Sprint Backlog during the Sprint Planning Meeting. If the Development Team chooses to do more than they figure they can handle, or if they overestimate the ability to get things done, that will lead down one of two roads.

The first road is to work overtime. Now, if the team can handle it, then it might not be such a big deal. But if the Development Team is not accustomed to handling heavy workloads, then they might end up running out of steam midway through the project or even at mid-sprint.

So, it is absolutely essential for the Scrum Master to assess their team's capabilities. It is always better to reduce the scope of the workload than to up the number of hours the team will be working. In addition, the Scrum Master needs to be aware of the complexity of the work being done. This is why the Scrum Master should, at the very least, have a theoretical understanding of the work being conducted. This understanding will enable the Scrum Master to counsel the developers as to what they can reasonably handle.

The Scrum Master is the member in charge of grooming the Sprint Backlog. The Scrum Master is also in charge of making sure that the work is being completed on schedule. In a manner of speaking, the Scrum Master is similar to the guy beating the drum on a rowboat. The purpose of beating the drum is not to demand more from the rowing team. Rather, the beating of the drum is done in order to establish a rhythm and pace for the rowers. As such, the Scrum Master needs to help the developers build a sustainable pace so that they can cross the finish line on schedule.

It is also important to note that one of the main outcomes of the Sprint Planning Meeting is the Sprint Goal. The Sprint Goal is a simple statement indicating what the team expects to get done during a specific sprint. That way, the customer can see how much progress the team has made during that particular sprint.

During the Sprint Retrospect Meeting, the entire Scrum team will go over the Sprint Goal and ultimately decide if the goal was met or not. If it was, then high-fives would be in order. If it wasn't, then lessons learned need to emerge from the understanding of what went wrong and how it could be improved.

Now, one important caveat to consider. Scrum encourages creativity and self-regulation the entire way. However, Development Teams are not encouraged to carry out tasks that they believe will enhance the features and functionalities of a product, especially if they haven't been requested by the customer. By doing additional tasks that have not been required, the team is essentially working for free.

But beyond working for free, doing tasks that were not initially included at the outset of the Sprint will take time away from other tasks to be done. An argument could be made regarding time left over, that is, if a task takes less time than anticipated.

So, if a team is ever left with time to spare, this is the time that needs to be devoted to testing. Even if the testing planned for that sprint has already been conducted, additional testing will only help to confirm that the deliverables are working as they should.

As a matter of fact, additional testing may lead to bugs that may have slipped through the cracks earlier in the Sprint. This is why testing cannot be stressed enough. So, whenever there is time left over, it ought to be devoted to testing. Otherwise, doing unsolicited work will only lead to frustration for the Development Team.

When a Scrum team is ready to showcase its progress at the Sprint Review Meeting, it is important to note that acceptance criteria need to be clearly defined. By "acceptance criteria," we are referring to the parameters that need to be met in order for the deliverables to safely pass the test.

Of course, the basis for acceptance criteria comes from the customer's expectations. After all, they have the final say in whether the sprint gets the green light or the heave-ho. Yet, the Development Team must also have its own set of acceptance criteria.

These criteria can come in the form of a checklist. This about it in this way: it is like a pre-flight checklist that needs to be covered before the plane can take off.

Here is a sample of what that checklist would look like:

- The functionalities are reviewed by a designated individual (i.e., Scrum Master) or even a project stakeholder.
- Testing is conducted to see if the product meets the requirements set forth at the beginning of the Sprint.

- All quality assurance testing completed
- —completion of any, and all, documentation related to the User Story (manuals, checklists, worksheets, and so on).
- Any, and all, issues, bugs, and issues corrected.
- Acceptance by the Customer at the Sprint Review Meeting.

When the customer gives the final thumbs-up, the Development Team is now ready to move on to the next sprint. However, if issues are brought up by the customer, then a change request may very well be issued. This change request may be something as simple as a change in the color scheme of an application, or the correction of an error seen during the demo of the deliverable. While to err is human, Scrum teams must strive toward eliminating as many errors as possible.

The successful completion of the sprint will clear that sprint's Backlog and subsequently take items off the

Product Backlog. When an item is officially "done," it is said that this is an "increment." In other words, an increment in the rise of work done or completed. Consequently, Scrum is an incremental methodology since it builds the final product as if it were building a brick wall. Each item completed in the Backlog is a brick that has been laid on the wall.

It is also important to keep in mind that while every sprint needs to deliver "working software" to the customer, that doesn't necessarily mean that the product is ready for release. In fact, it might mean that the product is working, but it is not ready to be released yet. As a matter of fact, most beta testing periods are an individual testing sprint that is conducted prior to an initial release.

In the example about designing a car, the car may very well be fully operational, that is, a driver can sit inside and take it for a ride. But since the entire round of testing is yet to be completed, the Product Owner may choose to hold on to the car for one more sprint before holding its first release. So, a testing sprint may be conducted in which a test driver will take the car around the track for a few laps. This will enable the team to greenlight the car and release the first version.

Once the first version of the car is released, the manufacturer may give the nod for the car to be produced en masse. Subsequent model years would represent further releases, especially if the following model years correct issues that may have gone undetected during testing.

The last artifact that we are going to discuss is the Burndown Chart. At its core, the Burndown Chart is a graphic organizer that compares the tasks that need to be completed with the amount of time remaining in the sprint. So, at the beginning of the sprint, there will be 0% of work completed and 100% of the time available.

In order to make the Burndown Chart work effectively, the time allotted to that sprint needs to be broken down into equal blocks of time. So, let's assume the following scenario:

A Development Team has four weeks to complete one User Story in the Sprint. As such, the full User Story is the Sprint Goal. The Development Team has 20 working days at 8 hours apiece. In total, that's 160 hours, in which four team members must complete a total of 15 tasks.

So, one eight-hour workday represents 5% of the total time allotted to that sprint. In other terms, every hour represents $1/160^{th}$ of the time assigned to that sprint. As you can see, time is truly of the essence in Scrum.

Another key factor that plays into the calculation of the Burndown Chart is timeboxing. Timeboxing consists of assigning an estimated amount of time that a task will take. So, task #1 will is estimated to take a total of 10 hours. The goal is to complete the task within the amount of time set forth for it. This is where the Scrum Master must track the team's performance.

At the Daily Standup Meeting, the Scrum Master may call the team's attention to the fact that they might be running behind schedule. At that point, the team may choose to up the ante by working longer hours or coming in on weekends or decide to push a task to another sprint. However, if the task gets pushed back, care must be taken to ensure that it won't affect the deliverables being completed in that particular sprint.

In an ideal world, 100% of the work will be done in 100% of the time. However, practice and experience in-  dicate that this isn't always the case. Newer and less-experienced Scrum teams tend to fall behind. This may require additional efforts in order to meet deadlines.

Of course, the Burndown Chart is not set in stone. So that does not mean that tasks cannot be moved around or timeboxing altered. However, this is not the preferred course of action. The ideal course of action would be to get everything planned correctly so that modifications to the original plan are avoided.

At the end of the day, the artifacts in Scrum are intended to guide the work done by the Development Team. Otherwise, the Development Team would have no objective measure that would indicate if they are progressing as per the Sprint Backlog. Therefore, the Scrum Master's role is pivotal in beating that drum and making sure that the team is moving along at an even pace.

Ultimately, the goal of any Scrum team is to develop a sustainable pace in which they can work comfortably so that they can do what they have set out to do in the

amount of time they have to do it. That is why the artifacts of Scrum serve as a means of gauging performance and fine-tuning any components that need to
be tuned.

Chapter 6

THE APPLICATIONS OF
SCRUM METHODOLOGY

Scrum has been generally typecast in the software industry. To most common observers, Scrum was developed for the IT industry as a whole. And while it is
true that Scrum was born from the software and IT
industries, it is also true that it can be applied to virtually all areas of work. Now, this doesn't mean that
Scrum is some type of universal methodology that can
cure all ills. What it does mean is that Scrum has the
flexibility to be implemented across various industries.
So, in this chapter, we are going to take a closer look
at how Scrum can be deployed in various scenarios.

The first, and obvious, the use of Scrum is in IT. Virtually all of the large software and IT corporations have made use of some type of Agile methodology at some point. Microsoft used Extreme Programming back in the way while Google, Facebook, and Apple are all known to have deployed Scrum at various points.

The fact of the matter is that Scrum is a good fit in this area since the projects conducted by these companies are highly experimental. What that means is that they often develop products and services that did not exist at one point in recent history.

A good example of this is Apple and its venerable iPhone. When the iPhone debuted in 2007, there had been nothing like it in this past. It was a revolutionary design, much like Blackberry had been before that. As such, these types of products deal in areas where there are very few, if any, comparable products. Project engineers need to think on their feet and come up with some means of developing the best means of reaching their objective.

That being said, the iPhone was not developed using Scrum, but it simply goes to show that high levels of uncertainty require a great degree of flexibility and adaptability. This also means that project teams need to be aware of how things may rapidly take shifts in different directions. Therefore, traditional project management methodologies fall short when addressing the very nature of change.

Other companies such as Philips, General Electric, Nokia, and Siemens have been known to use Scrum in various projects. As a result, more and more companies within the tech sector have been embracing the use of Scrum as a viable project management methodology.

Outside of the world of technology, Scrum is yet to gain a significant foothold. The reason for this is that many corporations have been using traditional methodologies such as the Waterfall approach for far longer. Therefore, it is not easy for corporations to do away with tried and tested methodologies even when there is a viable alternative that has slowly proven to be superior in many ways.

It is interesting to note that Toyota was the first corporation to use an Agile approach in its manufacturing process. Toyota first came up with the concept of "Kanban" back in the late 1970s. Kanban literally means "card" in Japanese. It was devised as a means of streamlining communication before means of communication such as mobile phones were even on the horizon. The Kanban system worked so well for Toyota that it began spreading across other corporations. To this day, virtually all manufacturing process uses some type of Kanban procedure.

This example goes to illustrate that Agile has always been on the minds of companies that are looking to innovate. Hence, Scrum has become very well received among startups and smaller companies that are looking to disrupt larger incumbents. Ultimately, the use of Agile leads to innovation, creativity, and profitability due to one core reason: developers are given a chance to use their talents without interference from "know-it-alls." As such, Scrum developers don't receive orders. They act according to their knowledge, talent, and expertise.

Consequently, any company that is looking to innovate their current processes, no matter how "perfect" they might be, can look to Scrum as an alternative throughout their innovation process. Scrum can provide the flexibility that a traditional approach cannot.

So, let's go back to the first example we discussed at the outset of this book: road construction.

In this example, we pointed out how road construction is the kind of project that has a much lower change and uncertainty when compared to other types of projects. As such, the use of traditional project management methodologies would suit this type of project just fine.

However, let's add a new twist. What if we were to use Scrum as part of a road construction project? What would that look like?

First of all, the project would have to be broken down into sprint. Depending on the length of the road being built, the project team could break down the road into 10 km segments, or 5-mile increments. At the outset of each sprint, the Development Team would have to come together and determine what User Story would be addressed. Given the fact that virtually anyone would be using this road, the Development Team would have to deal with several User Stories.

Consequently, each sprint would only partially address the User Story. The end result would be achieved once the entire road has been completed. Once the sprint is done, the stakeholders can come together to have a look at the stretch of road that has been finished. Cars can test drive the road to see if it meets the standards required for such projects. Once that stretch of the road gets the thumbs up, the Development Team can move on to the next portion of a road.

In this example, it is safe to assume that the Development Team will not consist of four to six members. In fact, it may consist of hundreds of workers. Given the possible size of the Development Team, the Product Owner might have to make a decision, either field on massive Scrum team divided up into sections, or perhaps have several Development Teams working in synch. This is a question that we will be discussing in greater depth later on. For now, it's worth mentioning that the size of the team can be a big as it needs to be in order to get the job done.

Another example of how Scrum can be deployed in other areas comes from the film industry.

Traditionally, films are produced in a very Scrum-like manner. Rather than being shot from beginning to end in the sequence that the script is written, films are shot in a manner similar to a puzzle. Then the post-production process put the various scenes together. During this post-production process, many errors and inconsistencies are picked up. In some of the worst cases, entire scenes need to be reshot after the fact. Naturally, this something that all film directors want to avoid.

So, Scrum is a perfect fit for the film industry. Each sprint can represent a logical portion of the movie. For example, if the movie is set in several locations, each sprint can take place in each location. Also, each sprint can represent the major scenes in the film, thereby giving it the logical sequencing that the sprint requires.

After each sprint, the film team can produce a rough version of what the film would like. So, rather than having one big premiere for studio executives, the film team can produce smaller "mini-premieres." This would give the studio executives a good idea of where the movie is headed.

All of the post-production aspects of the film can become part of a quality assurance/testing sprint. In this manner, the project team can ensure that the film meets all of the acceptance criteria set forth by the stakeholders.

Once the film is completed, it is ready for the final release. By this time, everyone can be certain that the film meets all of the criteria. In addition, it virtually eliminates the possibility of undetected errors popping up. Thus, there won't be any risk of plot holes, inconsistencies, or mistakes that fans usually pick up on.

As a matter of fact, television shows follow this approach.

Before a new show is added to a network's line up, a pilot is produced. This pilot is a demo of what the actual show will look like. Then, audiences review the pilot in a type of focus group. This data helps network executives green light a show or ax it.

In the end, a television show is produced in sprints. Except each sprint is called a "season." Television shows are also produced with a specific type of audience in mind very similar to the way a User Story would be crafted. If the show is a hit, it means the project team got it right. If it flops, then the project team needs to go back to the drawing board and figure out what went wrong.

Of course, television shows don't typically deploy Scrum as their working methodology, but this example serves to show that the iterative nature of production exists in some of the places you would least imagine. In the case of television shows, that's exactly what they do. They craft a formula that works and then replicate it for as long as audiences find it amusing.

Now, if you thought those were the only examples of non-IT industries where Scrum could be deployed, the guess again. There are plenty of other examples in which Scrum can be put to the test. And some of these areas might surprise you.

So, let's discuss fashion design — yes, fashion.

In the fashion industry, the creation of new products and designs often pushes into uncharted territory. Fashion brands that do not strive to innovate on a consistent basis often end up missing out on opportunities to capitalize on their market share because they cannot produce designs that would differentiate them from the rest of the competition.

That being said, a fashion brand could very well deploy Scrum to produce a new collection of items. The brand can divide their products up into various categories based on the User Stories created. Each User Story would represent the type of market they are looking to capture. For instance, if they are looking to capture a younger audience, the brand might choose to have one or two User Stories, or multiple ones, depending on the type of person their products are being marketed for.

Each of the sprints would address the User Stories created with the ultimate unveiling of the finished product at an officially sanctioned fashion show. The specifics of each sprint would depend on what resources the company has to work in terms of time and money. In the end, the project team would be able to develop an iterative process since they wouldn't need to produce all of the articles at the same time. Rather, they could develop certain groups or articles, and even conduct focus group reviews or any other type of feedback in order to gauge how the market would ultimately react to their upcoming collection.

Up to now, we have looked at some examples of how Scrum could be deployed in non-IT industries. These examples seem to naturally lend themselves to the use of Scrum, but what about an industry that doesn't necessarily lend itself to Scrum?

There is any number of industries in which you wouldn't necessarily think that Scrum could be implemented. Nevertheless, Scrum could certainly be put to good use regardless of the industry itself. Let's have a look at a couple of such examples.

The financial services industry (banks, investment institutions, insurance brokers, and so) often deal with high degrees of uncertainty. In these situations, financial institutions need to be on their toes. After all, anyone familiar with the way this type of business works will tell you that if you blink, you might end up losing your shirt.

With that in mind, the financial services industry can break down its operations into User Stories. So, if a large investment bank serves ultra-wealthy individuals who have a net worth of over 5 million dollars, then this User Story would need to reflect the profile for that type of customer.

By the same token, if the investment institution is going after the average investor and not ultra-wealthy, then the User Story would need to reflect. What if they are going after both? Then, there needs to be multiple User Stories used to address this nature.

Next, the financial institution can deploy Scrum to build investment products which it will then offer to its customers. It should be noted that we are talking about creating products and services which the institution will offer its customers. We are not implying that Scrum can be used as a methodology for running day to day operations. While Scrum could be used as a permanent management approach, the use of Scrum is more intended and building a portfolio of products that a financial institution can offer its customers.

Once the project team has assembled the products and services that it feels will address the needs of its customers, the institution can then implement these products and services during a testing phase. During this testing phase, the institution can gauge to see if the products have performed up to their own expectations and those of their customers. If the products happen to fall short for some reason, there is room for improvement. Otherwise, a final release can be conducted, and the products and services are officially rolled out to the public.

In this example, a financial institution would be able to shift its focus from a process-oriented approach to a customer-centered one. In that manner, the financial institution can draft User Stories in order to put a name and face to the customers they are striving to acquire. After all, if a company does not have a clear vision on whom they are attempting to serve, their endeavors may fall short of delivering the type of value their customers seek.

Now, let's consider how Scrum could be deployed in a manufacturing context.

Manufacturing is very process-oriented; that is, manufacturers are always looking to improve their processes in order to reduce the number of defects and the amount of problems that may arise during the production of goods.

As such, Scrum doesn't immediately jump out as a viable alternative in this area. However, Scrum, with its iterative nature, actually makes a great deal of sense.

When the beneficiary of a process is clearly defined, it is easy to implement Scrum in such a way that the beneficiary is the recipient of the end result of the Scrum deliverables. Think about it in this manner: rather than developing process and tools which require individuals to be trained in their use (thereby requiring companies to find workers who may, or may not, possess the qualities they are looking for), a manufacturer would build the process and tools around the workers they do have.

For instance, a factory has been having trouble finding workers because they lack some type of skill, such as a high degree of computer skills. So, the company has decided to shift its focus from building a process that requires workers to have skills that they do not have, and the manufacturer has decided to alter its processes in such a manner that it can play off the strengths their workers do have.

In this example, the end-user is not the customer who purchases the products that are rolled out of the assembly line. Rather, the end-user is the worker who is on the factory floor carrying out the processes devised by process engineers. What this does is that it reduces reliance on skills and expertise, which may be in short supply and focuses on the more abundant and readily available skill sets.

This particular situation underscores one of the points contained in the Agile Manifesto pertaining to valuing people over processes. Any time companies value their people over processes and documentation; the shift then focuses on how to get the most out of the people already on board. Hence, creating a User Story that reflects the type of worker a company needs is actually a great way of helping recruiters figure out who they need to get.

Of course, recruiters have a wish list of qualities and skills that they would like to find in every candidate they interview. Yet, some of these skills or traits may not be readily available. So, companies need to figure out who they've got on hand and tailor their processes to suit the strengths of the folks who are out there.

If a company puts processes over people, it would be like creating a product and then expecting customers to change their consumption habits to suit that type of product. If a product somehow doesn't mesh with a person's usual patterns of consumption, the chances of them buying the product are slim.

That is why companies need to figure out what customers want and deliver that value.

In the same manner, companies need to figure out the type of workers that are available to them and playoff those strengths. Naturally, there are skill sets that cannot be negotiated. For example, workers are required to speak English; otherwise, they would be unable to communicate. But assuming that a company operates in a company where skilled labor that is fluent in English is in short supply, the company could deploy Scrum to figure out how it can use the strengths of the people they do have.

Often times, this creative thought process leads to unexpected results. Currently, more and more companies are using artificial intelligence in cases where it can reasonably use code to replace a person. This is a way to get around a lack of language skills while delivering 24/7 customer support.

At the end of the day, Scrum can be deployed in virtually any type of industry and context. However, the most glaring obstacle for Scrum deployment may lie in the mindset of project managers out there. Some are either unfamiliar with the way Scrum could be implemented in their line of work, or they are too set in their ways. As such, it is important for you, who are reading this, to keep an open mind and determine how Scrum could benefit your company, and your life for that matter.

Chapter 7

TEAM MECHANICS IN SCRUM

Perhaps the biggest reason why Scrum fails to deliver is the fact that Scrum practitioners are unable to transmit the Agile mindset in an effective manner. What this means is that all of the members of a team need to be sold on the effectiveness of Scrum, and what they are doing is a good way of developing value to their customers.

Think about it along these lines: on a sports team, if the players are not sold on working collectively toward helping the team win, their efforts won't reflect a winning attitude on the field. In fact, you may have a collection of players who are only out there for themselves thinking about their next contract.

In such cases, a team is destined to fail because of the lack of commitment from all players. Just like 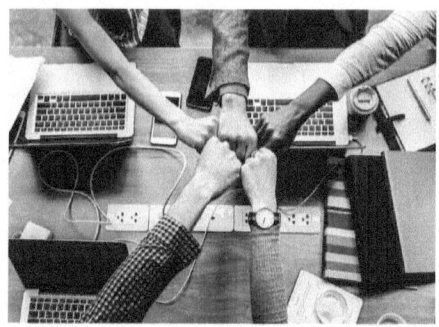 in a sports team, Scrum needs to have fully committed players in order for it to be truly effective. If the collection of players on the team is only working for a paycheck, then there might end up being suboptimal results. So, this chapter will take a look at how team mechanics are crucial to implementing Scrum effectively.

Now, the first, and most important thing, to keep in mind is the Agile mindset. While the Agile mindset might harmless enough on paper, it might prove to be a rather different manner of working when compared to traditional methodologies. This is especially true if team members are used to working in a pyramid-style of hierarchy.

As such, the first thing to keep in mind is that Scrum has a flat organizational structure. What this means is that each member has their own role. Also, none of the roles are more important than others. After all, Scrum developers could not work properly without a Product Owner; the Product Owner could not do their job without the Development Team, the Scrum Master would be lost without the Development Team, and so on.

This interdependency creates a natural workflow that enables everyone to focus on their job and to get the results that are expected of them. Nevertheless, a flat organizational structure doesn't mean that there isn't any room for leadership. In fact, Scrum encourages collaborative leadership in such a way that everyone takes a turn leading the team depending on the tasks at hand.

Think of a cycling team. Cyclists take turns leading their teammates for a good reason. The speed at which they ride creates a headwind that increases the wind resistance of the cyclists at the front. Naturally, this means that the cyclists at the front will have to work harder in order to maintain their speed. Considering the headwinds, maintaining a fast pace would be unsustainable. So, while one team member breaks the headwinds, the rest fall back and take advantage of their teammate's efforts. Then, after a reasonable amount of time, another teammate moves to the front and takes on the headwinds.

In Scrum, this is the natural order of things. Some team members are more naturally suited to face some headwinds than others. This is the best way in which everyone has the chance to lead, and while avoiding putting unnecessary stress and pressure on single individuals.

Another important aspect of team mechanics in Scrum is responsibility.

Given the fact that there is no "authority" in a Scrum team, responsibility is spread out among the team members. This is important to keep in mind because the burden of the project's success or failure is not on one person's shoulders. This is something that traditional project managers have to deal with all the time.

When the burden of responsibility is placed on a single person, the amount of stress that an individual has to face can be tremendous. Consequently, traditional project managers may have a hard time coping with the expectations and demands of a project.

By the same token, those working under the project manager may feel that they have little, or no say, in the way things are done. This may end up creating feelings of resentment among team members as they feel they have a voice that deserves to be heard.

That is why Scrum does away with "authority" and advocates for leadership. Just like the previous example of the cycling team, leadership in Scrum is meant to be shared by everyone. By the same token, responsibility is also meant to be shared. Therefore, if the project is a success, everyone deserves the kudos. If the project fails, then everyone should be accountable for their shortcomings. Even when there is a clear point of failure in a project, that is, one team member is clearly responsible for the problem, there is no reason to point the finger at a single person.

In fact, a good Scrum team would foster an environment in which the responsible party would own up to their mistake, but it would also open a discussion to see what others could have done in order to support their teammate or prevent the mistake from happening.

This is a great example of sharing responsibility.

A situation such as this would be like a basketball team giving up a critical three-pointer, but rather than blaming one of the players for not covering the shooter, the players would ask themselves what they did, or didn't do, that enabled the shooter to get open and make the three-pointer.

When a team is willing to own up to their mistakes in a collective fashion, it reduces the amount of stress placed on a single person as it allows the entire team to take responsibility for their individual role. The fact is that most people enjoying having responsibility, that is, knowing that what they are doing is meaningful and their voice is heard every step of the way. Eventually, natural leaders will become adept at giving fewer outgoing members the opportunity to take the lead when they feel comfortable doing so.

One of the elements that Scrum pushed heavily on is having co-located teams. By "co-located," we are referring to having team members in the same physical location as much as possible. What this means is that a Scrum ought to be together, in the same physical place, at the same time.

What does that imply?

It implies that Scrum tries to avoid building virtual teams or having team members located in various points communicating only via digital means. Of course, modern technology has made it easier for team members to be located in various parts of the world. This means that if one individual with a specific skill set is not physically located in the same city as other team members, technology can enable this person to work remotely.

While it is true that remote working has gained a lot of momentum in recent years, and it seems to have quickly become a viable alternative for many companies, the fact of the matter is that Scrum works best when teams are able to work together in the same place, at the same time.

This approach fosters constant collaboration while it allows issues to be addressed in a face to face manner as opposed to dealing with things on separate terms.

When a team is remotely located, there many challenges that the project team must deal with.

First of all, different time zones can be a real productivity killer. There are instances when even a one- or two-hour-time difference can become a significant hurdle to overcome. This is common with teams that have members in the Eastern Standard Time Zone and the Pacific Standard Time Zone. While a couple of hours may not seem like a big deal, it is enough to make a meeting, discussion, and collaboration hard enough.

This problem is magnified when teams are located in different countries and in completely different time zones. As such, a team split up between America and Asia may find it extremely difficult to work together efficiently. If you have ever dealt with customers and partners located halfway around the world, then you have a keen insight into how this condition can potentially become disruptive.

Therefore, co-located teams reduce the amount of time that is lost in translation, that is, the time that is lost attempting to come up with schedules that suit everyone's particular situation. While it might be easy for a team to set a time for the Daily Standup Meeting in stone, someone is certain to get the short end of the stick. For instance, one team member might log on to the meeting a 3 pm while another might log on a 3 am.

Another important aspect to consider when working with remote teams is internet reliability.

Internet reliability is something that is not always taken into consideration until it becomes an issue. For most remote jobs, having a stable internet connection is fundamental. However, there are countries in which internet service isn't quite as reliable as in North America or Europe.

Ultimately, this lack of connectivity can make it very disruptive to effective team mechanics. If a team member consistently misses the Daily Standup Meeting, for instance, it may lead to a good deal of miscommunication. And given Scrum's nature, having interaction throughout the sprint is vital to ensuring the achievement of outcomes.

After all, it's not quite the same to have a face to face talk, even if it's over Skype or FaceTime, as it is to read an email with several bullet points. In addition, most folks don't have the time nor the attention span to read copious amounts of information in an email.

Also, a live chat functionality, while certainly useful and timesaving at times, it can prove to be disruptive to productivity when large amounts of information need to be transmitted. Furthermore, if the team decides to hold calls over conventional landline telephones or mobile phones, the phone bills at the end of the month may end up forcing the company to go bankrupt.

Indeed, virtual teams may be a good solution if various conditions coincide. If time zones and internet reliability are not a significant issue, then going for a virtual team might an option, especially if there aren't any physical objects being built. However, if the team is producing a physical object, that is, something which you can hold in your hands, then it might be best to go the co-located route.

Some large, multinational corporations do find logic in working remotely as they might have their various headquarters spread out throughout the world. As such, the company already has experts on board who can carry out the activities set forth in the project, but because they might be located in various parts of the world, every team member may need to make a bit of a sacrifice for the greater good.

In this case, corporations have to make a choice: utilize internal talent who knows everything about the company and the project at the expense of some comforts or bring in a team that can work in a co-located fashion in one specific schedule. Either alternative seems like they are giving up something to get something.

However, there is a third option: pull project members out of their regular jobs and devote them exclusively to the project. This approach has provided mixed results as it implies travel for some, work piling up for others, and temporary replacements for practically all of them.

Then again, a corporation might consider bringing external consultants to carry out a Scrum-based project. It is certainly feasible, especially if the consultants have the experience and know-how in producing the deliverables the corporation needs. In such cases, the corporation might name a staff member as Product Owner while the consulting company furnishes the Scrum Master and developers.

In the end, companies need to figure out which configuration works best for them. In this regard, there might be some trial and error happening before consistent and sustainable team mechanics can be developed. That way, the team can find a happy medium, thereby ensuring their long-term success.

An often-overlooked aspect of Scrum team mechanics is the team's official working language. Now, this shouldn't be an issue if everyone speaks the same language. However, things can get a bit tricky when you have folks that don't speak the same native language.

Generally speaking, the default language for Scrum is English. Virtually all documentation is available in English, while relevant training aids are primarily produced for English speakers. There have been efforts to produce materials in other languages. This has suited training purposes just fine. But what happens when the actual work being conducted is done by folks who don't have the same level of linguistic proficiency?

Most organizations that work with team members from various countries and locations will establish English as the default working language. However, not everyone might have the same level of English proficiency. This may lead to some communication problems, especially when a discussion gets highly technical.

Sure, the easiest way might be to find professionals who already have a good level of English proficiency. But such professionals might not be quite as easy to find. In fact, highly qualified professionals who speak English fluently are not that easy to find.

If a project team does not necessarily need to produce deliverables in English, the language might be a moot point. However, the overarching issue to consider is communication. After all, communication is pivotal in ensuring that a project gets done well and with as little obstacles as possible.

One area that might be of concern is documentation not available in the team's native language. In general, technical documentation is available in English but may not be available in other languages. If this proves to be an obstacle for the team, the Scrum Master might have to drill down and do some homework in order to help the team fully comprehend the information. Otherwise, translation services may have to be factored into the requirements for the project. In that case, the Product Owner may go about looking for a translator who could help the team get the right information they need in a timely manner.

Overall, language might become an issue if the team cannot seem to communicate effectively. Nevertheless, language only becomes a real obstacle when the entire team cannot rally around a common language. Since language is often overlooked, it may pop up as an unforeseen issue at some point. But since Scrum is highly flexible, adjustments can be made in the upcoming sprint in order to address these complications and ensure that everything runs smoothly for the remainder of the project's lifespan.

The last item in this discussion pertains to pace.

Earlier, we brought up the point about the need for a sustainable pace. By "sustainable pace," we are referring to a workflow in which the team feels comfortable and is highly productive. Consequently, the exact definition of "sustainable" can vary greatly.

The biggest reason for differing valuation of the term "sustainable" has to do with the fact that not all teams are created equal. By that measure, some teams can work longer hours and at a faster pace than others. Other teams may work at a slower tempo but produce greater quality results.

Ultimately, the pace, or tempo, with which a team works essentially boils down to the individuals themselves. If team members are not used to working under pressure, this may motivate the Product Owner and Scrum Master to choose a slower tempo in order to avoid burning out the team.

On the other hand, if the team members enjoy a high-octane pace, then pushing the envelope a bit more might certainly be within the realm of possibility. The fact of the matter is that this is entirely up to the team members. It can also be challenging for a Scrum Master who is unfamiliar with the way an individual team reacts to pressure.

So, a good rule of thumb is to start off slow and ramp up the pace depending on how the team reacts. Furthermore, the Development Team will have to decide at which points they can floor it, and at which points they will need to pull back. This is a crucial consideration since there are parts of a project that don't necessarily present many complications. However, there are other parts of a project which may require greater attention to detail give the nature of the tasks at hand.

This is why the term "sustainable" does not necessarily refer to an even tempo throughout the project but certainly throughout the sprint. In fact, work can be planned-out in such a way that the team may choose to frontload most of the heavy lifting while leaving the remaining sprints a bit less intense. Or, the team may choose to alternate between heavy sprints and less intense ones.

Ultimately, this is a decision that the entire Development Team needs to make. The Scrum Master does not have the authority to push the team to do more and more. If that were the case, then the Scrum Master would not be fulfilling their role as per Scrum guidelines.

Now, there is one important consideration: if the team were to fall behind, for whatever reason, the time might be tempted to make up for the lost time. This is especially important if there is a hard deadline that cannot be extended by any means. In that case, the team may just have to suck it up. However, great care needs to be taken not to overextend the team. Burnout is a real thing and can cause a team to become far less productive than they should. So, the team does fall behind. The best way to make up for lost time would be to find a way to accommodate the workflow so that the team can meet its targets. The one task that a Development Team should always try to avoid cutting back on is testing. This is the most important task the team can do since it will ensure that everything is working the way it's supposed to.

Chapter 8

SECRETS OF HIGH PERFORMANCE TEAMS

The business world is filled with literature about improving team performance. In most cases, such literature is a collection of well-meaning advice that doesn't lead anywhere. On other occasions, this literature contains information that doesn't apply to a team, such as a Scrum project team. In this chapter, we are going to take a look at ways in which Scrum teams can improve performance and get the most out of their tenure in a project.

The first thing to consider in this chapter is the following: what is a high-performance team?

There are many sides to this question, as it is open to interpretation. For some, high-performance means a heightened level of productivity, that is, getting more done in less time. Period When a team is working under this directive, you have to question the quality of the work being put forth. That is, is the team really getting more done in less time? Or are they simply going through the motions regardless of the quality of the outcome?

When a team's mandate is to get things done as quickly as possible, there is always the temptation to cut corners as much as possible. When a project leader allows their team to cut corners, then the outcome will become uncertain. There is no guarantee that the outcome will conform to expectations. Furthermore, when a team is willing to sacrifice quality, they end up costing the customer a lot more time and money, especially if mistakes are made along the way.

Indeed, working against the clock is one of the most common aspects of project development. However, a balance needs to be found between getting things done as swiftly as possible and with the quality that customers expect.

This is why the first point for developing high-performance teams is understanding the project's scope. Often, the scope of a project can get lost in the shuffle simply because the project leader doesn't understand what the customer really wants. This may lead the project team to focus on tasks and functionalities that don't really match up with what the customer wants.

So, for the sake of getting things done, especially when there is a tight turnaround, understanding the project scope becomes essential. In this case, a Product Owner needs to sit down and clearly interpret what the customers want. Many times, this is a skill that is honed over time. Nevertheless, it is crucial for a Product

Owner to have a keen understanding of what the customer is looking to achieve.

When the Product Owner has a clear vision, it is easier for the entire team to translate that into a working product that can meet the expectations of the customer and comply with the objectives set forth at the outset of the project.

But, how can a Product Owner interpret the customer's desires?

That can be tricky, especially if the customer doesn't really know what they want. This is, perhaps, the biggest obstacle a project team can face. When the customer is unclear about what they really want to get out of a project, they will have a hard time articulating that vision.

Therefore, it is the job of the Product Owner to offer the customer a concise proposal that can help them meet their needs. Of course, there is always the desire to offer a product with all the bells and whistles, but frankly speaking, how important are all those bells and whistles? This is why the product that delivers on what the customer really wants is the most important thing any Product Owner can do in order to ensure that the project will come in on time and under budget.

The second thing that high-performance teams do is communicate.

Now, you might be thinking: all management books talk about communication.

That is true. But most management books don't focus on communication among Scrum team members. Communication in a Scrum project should be as direct and clear as possible. No frills. The team needs to articulate what they need, express their concerns, and get the message across without sugarcoating anything.

The reason for advocating a communication strategy of this nature lies in the fact that there is no time to  waste. Sure, socializing and bonding are fundamental. But there is a time for that. There is time for having a drink after work and getting to know your teammates better.

When you're on the clock, it is important to get the message across when you need to. For example, the Daily Standup Meeting allots 15 minutes to discuss the day's matters. This means that each team member needs to get their information across in a matter of minutes. Those team members that like to give speeches may need to rethink their approach.

The fact is that all team members need to focus consistently. This can be tough, especially when team members are new to Scrum. It can be tough to focus specifically on the task at hand. Nevertheless, it is a necessary skill.

So, how can you develop quick and effective communication?

One of the Scrum Master's tasks is to collect information about the project. This information gathering process is focused on determining what is actually happening in the project so that they can be proactive in any issues that might come up. If a Scrum Master shows up at the Daily Standup Meeting with a small agenda in mind, there will be no chance to waste time.

Also, the Daily Standup Meeting should be conducted standing up, as all meetings should. The reason behind this approach lies in the fact that if people get comfortable, they will be more likely to spend a good deal of time talking. Needless to say, this is not the best approach to take during meetings.

It should also be noted that Scrum teams only have the Daily Standup Meeting as an official meeting event. There are no Monday morning meetings to talk about the week ahead. There are no impromptu sessions to go over something that has popped into the Scrum Master's mind. There is also no other type of interaction in which the team is able to take time away from productive working time for the sake of a meeting.

In short, meetings are not considered productive.

One more thing: lunch and coffee breaks need to be worked in addition to productive time. So, that means that if a team is going to work eight hours a day, that means working eight hours a day. Lunch and break should be tacked on to the productive time. Thus, a team may spend nine hours at the office, but actually working eight. If the project team has an official work schedule of eight hours but takes an hour and a half of that for lunch and breaks, then they are really working six and a half hours a day.

The point is not that a team must work eight hours. The point is that whatever the team agrees to work on a daily basis should be that. Anything else ought to be added to their usual work schedule.

With that in mind, the next element of high-performance teams is time management. Time management is an essential part of getting things done on time and within budget. However, most time management gurus look at this topic from an esoteric point of view, meaning that effective time management is somehow some elusive trait that only the enlightened can develop.

The truth is that time management is the type of skill anyone can develop. Nevertheless, it takes time and a bit of work to cultivate it.

The first element to effective time management is understanding the task at hand. This harkens back to the point about the bells and whistles of a project. While it is tempting to give customers more than they expect, the customer will not be willing to pay more for that, nor will they be willing to wait longer. A customer will be perfectly happy with getting what they are paying for.

Thus, any team member needs to be absolutely clear about what they are doing. If they know exactly what needs to be done, then that is what they need to deliver. Think about it like this: if you are painting a room, you will paint the room using the color paint the customer has asked for. Then, you paint the four walls and you are done. But what if you decide to paint the room as if it were the Sistine Chapel? Sure, the customer will be pleased to see that you've gone the extra mile—if you can do it within the same time frame and at no extra cost. But if this means overrunning cost and time for the project, then the customer won't be too pleased.

The second element to effective time management is knowing why you are doing something. You might be the best at what you do, but if you don't understand why you are doing something, the likelihood of losing focus increases exponentially.

When an individual does not have a clear understanding of why they are doing something, they will begin to question every aspect of the task they are carrying out. This will lead to a significant amount of stress simply because the final outcome is unclear.

The military is a great example of this. Even when soldiers go into a top-secret mission, they are often fed information on a "need to know basis." What this means is that they are told just enough so that they understand why they are going into harm's way. If soldiers don't understand why they are being deployed into battle, they are most likely to stay out of trouble rather than risking their lives in order to achieve the desired outcome.

While Scrum teams aren't necessarily putting their life in jeopardy, they might be putting their livelihood on the line. This is true, especially when their paycheck is dependent upon the successful completion of a project.

That is why the Product Owner and Scrum Master must make sure that every developer knows what they are doing and why they are doing it. If a developer is just going through the motions waiting for their paycheck at the end of the week, then it might be time to think about finding someone who is committed to the cause.

Given the fact that Scrum advocates for a collaborative approach, the Scrum Master needs to make sure that all developers know that their work, when put together, will add up to build the outcome the customer expects. This entails that individualities won't cut it.

There are no superstars. Scrum teams are not built around one superstar who is the face of the franchise. The team is built around a collection of individual players who can all deliver at the same level.

Consequently, outlining project objectives, the customer's expectations, and the Project Vision contribute to helping the Scrum team understand why they are doing what they are going. Otherwise, it might be hard to get everyone in the fold.

The third element to high-performance teams is trust.

In order to illustrate trust, let's go back to the example of the military. When soldiers are ordered to deploy, they need to trust that their commander is sending them out into battle for a good reason. If solders question their commanders' motives or simply don't believe their commander is capable of making the right decisions, then soldiers will hesitate when going out into the fray.

The underlying issue at this point is trust. If a solder trusts their commander, they will do what they are asked to the best of their abilities. The same goes for Scrum teams. Sure, there is no commander ordering anybody to do anything. After all, everyone is on the team out of their own free will. But the fact is that if a Scrum team trusts that the Project Vision laid out by the Product Owner is right, they will gladly get to work. But if they question what the Project Vision is, then this might lead to issues that can fester over time.

Now, does that mean that the Development Team should take everything the Product Owner says at face value and not question it? Hardly!

In fact, there is plenty of room for feedback from the Development Team. The Development Team can give both the Product Owner and Scrum Master their take on the way things are going and the way things ought to be done. If anything, having this active feedback is important to make sure that things are done as best they can.

When the Product Owner is open to suggestions from the team, they can even take those ideas back to the customer so that they can see why certain things are being done in that manner and why they are beneficial to the project's outcome.

When a team is able to talk among themselves within an environment of trust, then there will be very little room for issues to get out of hand. Please keep in mind that trust is a two-way street. Those who wish to be trusted must trust the other party in turn. Trust should be the default setting in a Scrum project until it is broken.

One of the most common issues that arise in any project is disagreements. So, how can a team handle a disagreement? What can they do when they arise? How can they solve differences in such a way that they don't interfere with the project itself?

Firstly, when there is trust, it is easy to talk about things. It is easy to discuss why there are differences and how these can be solved. For instance, if the product team believes that developing a functionality would take too long and thereby push up against the project's deadline, but the Product Owner insists that it is within the customer's expectations, they the team must find a way to figure out how it can be done.

If there really is no way of working it out, the Product Owner may choose to call an audible and push that task back to another sprint. That way, the team can work on other tasks that they feel will keep the chains moving while the Product Owner works out a solution to the difference of opinion.

That being said, both the Scrum Master and the Product Owner shouldn't be too actively involved in the way the Development Team actually conducts their tasks. That is, there is no reason why the Scrum Master or the Product Owner should be looking over the shoulder of each developer. They should be able to trust that they know how to do their job. In this manner, they won't have to sweat the details because they know that the work being conducted is being done as best as possible.

That leads to the final point about high-performance teams: having the right people on board.

Scrum is a no nonsense approach. Therefore, there is no time to be wasted, trying to figure things out. In order for a Scrum project to be as effective as it can possibly be, the right people, with the right know/how and the right experience, needed to be on board. This means that the selection process for team members needs to follow the project's scope as closely as possible.

What this entails is that the team ought to be comprised of people who understand what it will take to get the job done. Often, taking a flyer on someone who is inexperience may work out, but most of the time, it doesn't.

Now, it should be noted that inexperience doesn't apply to Scrum methodology; it applies to the technical knowledge needed to get the job done. Many times, giving someone a chance to learn on the job can lead to delays and costly mistakes. Of course, that doesn't mean that you can't give younger or inexperienced developers a shot. What it does mean is that if you have a team member who doesn't have much experience, surrounding them with mentors would certainly help keep things in balance.

But perhaps the most important aspect that you can look out for when bringing team members aboard is the right mindset. In short, people who are rigid, inflexible, and set in their ways may have a hard time adopting the Agile mindset.

Team members who are willing to adopt the Agile mindset are the kind of members who won't shy away from thinking outside the box and accepting that they don't know everything, no matter how smart and talented they are. Also, the Agile mindset calls for team members to work in an entirely collaborative manner. So, if there are team members who would rather work on their own, then you might have to reconsider having them on the team.

Lastly, the Agile mindset also calls for team members to be willing to share their knowledge and expertise with others. This means that all team members should feed each other in such a way that they can all help one another out when needed. For example, one developer may be struggling with a specific portion of their assigned tasks. This would be a good time for another team member to come in and help them out. Often, a collective head is much better at thinking than an individual one.

As you can see, developing a high-performance team does not contain any top-secret formulas. It all boils down to having the right attitude, which can then translate into the right mindset. When the entire team is moving in one direction, working toward a common outcome, and convinced that the way they are doing truly matters, then it won't be hard to get the job done. The main thing to keep in mind is that the sum of the parts of the team will always be greater than the individual components of the team.

Chapter 9

HOW TO RUN A SPRINT

Up to now, we have talked about the importance of effective team mechanics and the right mindset. So, now, it is time to focus on how all of these elements interact with one another in order to produce the desired outcomes within an individual sprint. If the team cannot develop the right rhythm within a sprint, it will be hard for the team to really get on track. That is why this chapter is focused on bringing all of the various components discussed throughout this book and integrating them into one solid system.

When the project is set to begin, there is a Project Vision and User Stories, which the team can work towards building. These two components will give the team the targets they need to shoot for. In this manner, there will be no doubt regarding what the team is looking to achieve.

So, the sprint officially begins with the Sprint Planning Meeting. The Sprint Planning Meeting is an event in which the entire team comes together to talk about the User Stories still on the board, and what needs to be done in order to meet the requirements of each one. In this regard, everyone has input in this process. Please bear in mind that this is not the Product Owner telling the team what they need to do. This is the Product Owner calling them team in, laying out the task at hand, and allow the Development Team to propose the best way they can find to get the job done.

As such, the Sprint Planning Meeting can take place over a morning and afternoon, during lunch, or at any time that suits the team best. During this time, the team should be able to find common ground and agree on what will be done, how it will be done, and who will do it.

Let's take a look at how this process can be carried out.

Suppose the project team is building a new video game. The User Stories reflect the type of person they believe will be interested in playing this game. As such, they will develop the functionalities that this user would like to see. One of those functionalities is a multiplayer, in-game communication capability. In short, users would like to be able to talk to each other during a multiplayer game.

So, the project team has come up with a way of how this can be done. Consequently, this task has been chosen as one of the tasks that will be included in the upcoming sprint. So, the first decision was to include it in the sprint — the next point to decide how the task will be broken down.

This is where the Development Team needs to agree on the breakdown for this particular task. This breakdown depends on the number of members on the team and the number of specific tasks that will be carried out. It could be that the development of this communication capability is comprised of hundreds of smaller tasks. By the same token, it could be that it is made up of several large tasks that need to be completed over several days of work.

In this regard, it is always best to let the Development Team figure out the best way to go about organizing themselves and completing the tasks. The last thing that both the Scrum Master and Product Owner want to do is try to "direct" or "organize" the workflow in a particular manner. They may offer their advice based on their experience and know-how, but ought to allow the developers to work out what makes them feel most comfortable.

It should be noted that a Sprint Planning Meeting isn't all that complicated. It can be a meeting that takes up a couple of hours. The most important aspect of this meeting is to be focused and avoid any distractions. Ideally, the Sprint Planning Meeting should take place the day before, or a couple of days before the beginning of the sprint. So, if the sprint is set to begin on a Monday morning, the Sprint Planning Meeting could take the place of the Saturday morning prior to the beginning of the sprint.

The chair of the Sprint Planning Meeting should be the Product Owner, especially during the first one for the project. Subsequent, meetings can be chaired by the Scrum Master. The role of the chair is just to direct discussing and bring the discussion back into focus, particularly if the conversation tends to veer off-topic. Beyond that, the Development Team should be free to discuss the items they feel are relevant to the upcoming sprint.

Once the workflow has been decided during the Sprint Planning Meeting, the team can begin to work on the actual sprint.

The sprint begins on the first day with the Daily Standup Meeting. During this meeting, the team members will simply inform one another of what will be done and what they expect to get done. This is just a means of bringing in the objectives of the day into focus.

As the work begins, the Development Team needs to be aware of the timeboxing allotted to each of the tasks set forth in that sprint. So, if one particular task is set to take up one hour, then it should be completed at that time.

As such, timeboxing is a means of helping each team member figure out how much time they should spend on a task. When teams don't time box their activities, they run the risk of losing focus and taking up far too long on a task. Then, they may find themselves trying to play catch up. A good way of time boxing activities is just to make a list of tasks and then to assign a number of hours next to it. This timeboxing exercise can then be contrasted with the Burndown Chart.

Now, the Burndown Chart doesn't rack individual tasks; all it does is track the overall time that the team has left in that sprint versus the amount of elapsed time. Each team member can then verify to see how many tasks they have left, the estimated time that they would need to complete them, and the time left in the sprint.

This type of administrative task is up to the Scrum Master to complete. That way, all the developers need to do is look at the chart and figure out how much time they have left during that sprint. If a developer happens to fall behind, for whatever reason, the Scrum Master can take a proactive approach and determine what they need in order to get back on track.

As the sprint progresses, the Scrum Master should hover around the team in the background, making sure that they have everything they need. Also, the Scrum Master ought to keep an eye on any potential issues that may arise.

Some examples of issues that may arise are supplies running out (printer ink, paper, markers, and such), equipment malfunctioning such as computers and printers, technical issues such as being unclear about coding or requirements made by the customer, and any unforeseen issues which may cause the team to run behind schedule.

In such projects where the team is using highly specialized or major equipment, the Scrum Master must make sure that everything in the running according to specifications. If the equipment begins to falter, the Scrum Master may seek out proactive corrective actions and deal with them as they arise. This might include preventive maintenance or even keeping spare parts around.

It is important to keep in mind that any issues that go beyond the scope of the Scrum Master's job need to be taken up with the Product Owner. For instance, there might be a need for additional purchases to be made. In this case, the Scrum Master ought to discuss the matter with the Product Owner so that the Product Owner can take it up with the client. If the Product Owner has the power to authorize the purchase or repair of equipment, then the Product Owner can go ahead and clear whatever acquisition needs to be made.

It should be noted that the developers need to be concerned with these matters. If they are shorthanded in terms of equipment, the Scrum Master must do their best to figure out an alternative solution until a permanent one can be found. So, if a laptop breaks down, a replacement one needs to be procured until the broken one can be fixed or a new one purchased. The aim here is to keep the project moving and avoid idle time as much as possible.

One important consideration that most Scrum practitioners have in the back of their minds, but don't really push for is what to do in the event that a team member is lost.

There are many reasons why a team member could be lost. For example, a team member can be placed on medical leave. They might simply quit or run into any situation which would hinder them from performing their job (there are many reasons why a developer would simply be unable to do their job).

As such, the Scrum Master needs to keep this potential situation in the back of their minds at all times. Failure to address this issue proactively may result in massive delays as a result of work backing up. Also, it might imply overloading the remaining members with tasks that may lead them to make mistakes. Consequently, it is best to avoid any kind of disruption.

One common solution is to have a bench, that is, an "extra" team member, or two, who could take on greater responsibility is need be. This "bench" serves the same purpose as bench players do in other sports.

Perhaps the best example is basketball. In basketball, there are five players on the court at all times. Yet, there is a bench of extra players that can come in at any point in the game. The only condition is that there must be a logical stoppage in play. They can't change on the fly, as happens in hockey. Plus, players can come in and out of the game as need be. This is different from baseball, where once a player leaves the game, they cannot come back into it.

So, some projects have one player who takes on less responsibility than the rest and is aware that whenever anything happens, they can be called up to supplant the missing player. This is an approach that seems to pay dividends, especially when the team is shorthanded. However, there are some negative elements to this approach.

One of the main drawbacks of this approach is the additional cost, which may, or may not, pay off in the long run.

Consider this situation: you need five developers but take on six because you feel that the sixth developer not only evens things out but also provides a buffer in case anyone should leave the team for any reason and for any length of time. Now, let's assume that everything is smooth sailing, and the job gets done well.

Does that justify carrying an extra team member? Some might argue that it lightened the load on everyone, while others may agree that it was an unnecessary cost that only affected the project's bottom line. As such, there needs to be a fine balance struck between cost and practicality.

Another potential drawback of this approach could be in the way the workflow is distributed. If the workflow is not evenly distributed among all members (including bench members), then those who have heavier loads may complain that they are working more than others (this problem is compounded when all members receive the same pay). Therefore, it is necessary to balance the workload with the understanding that one or more team members, maybe burdened with more work if anyone should leave the team.

In addition, bench members might feel that they are contributing less to the team when they are perfectly capable of bringing more to the table. In such cases, it is important to value everyone's contributions equally and provide them the opportunity to showcase their talents in a fair manner. So, this might mean distributing the workload in such a way that everyone knows they are doing less than they could, but also with the understanding that things could possibly tighten up at any given point.

Then, there is the question of payment. Do all members get equal remuneration even if some are doing more work than others?

Generally speaking, this shouldn't even be a question. Everyone should be compensated equally in order to avoid any potential issues with fair payment. However, what happens when things tighten up when the workload increases, but the payment doesn't?

Suppose that there are six team members all getting $10 an hour. But then, one team member leaves, and there are five members left doing the work that six used to do. Naturally, the workload increases, but the payment does not. Then, you might have a situation in which the remaining members might request for a raise.

This leads down two potential roads. One, stick with the five members for the rest of the project and give them a raise (possible $2 an hour each) or two, make it known that it is temporary until the other team member returns or a replacement is found.

Either way, it is important for both the Product Owner and Scrum Master to make these details clear when they are selecting their team members. Please bear in mind that the Agile mindset is always about going above and beyond the call of duty. While this doesn't mean that team members should be asked to do more than they were hired to do, it should be clear that in this situation, they may be asked to step up until a suitable alternative can be found.

Moreover, both the Product Owner and the Scrum Master ought to be aware that while a team member might very well leave mid-sprint, replacements should not be brought in mid-sprint, especially if they are un-familiar with Scrum methodology. They could be asked to join the team and observe the dynamic, but they wouldn't be asked to actually do anything until the next sprint begins. This will avoid upsetting the team's tempo as the sprint is in progress.

The question of team members leaving mid-sprint brings up one of the most controversial aspects of Scrum: the cancellation of a sprint.

There are two schools of thought on this: one says that a sprint should never be canceled and that every effort should be made to ensure that it keeps going despite hardships. The second school of thought believes that a sprint should be canceled if it is obvious that the objectives will not be met, or if the quality of the work will be so poor that it will surely fail to meet the customer's expectations.

So, let's consider the first school of thought.

Indeed, every effort needs to be made in order to ensure that the sprint keeps going despite hardships. After all, losing one team member is not catastrophic. However, losing two or three team members in one shot may very well be. In that case, the Scrum Master might consider finding replacements who can come through in a pinch, or perhaps hiring outside help. However, this is easier said than done.

First of all, replacements that can come in mid-sprint must be very experienced in the ways of Scrum and well-versed in the subject matter. Inexperienced people must never be brought in mid-sprint since the learning curve is not easy. Also, learning how to work on a Scrum project on the fly can be intimidating and even scary.

Secondly, asking the remaining members to suck it up and push through may lead the team to be burned out. This is especially true if members leave at the beginning of the sprint, and there is a lot to be done. It's all just a question of numbers.

For example, if there are five members, all working eight hours a day, that means that there are 40 working hours every day. But if two of the five members leave, that means that 40 hours suddenly get divided into three, leaving working days of roughly 13.5 hours for each member.

How sustainable do you think that would be?

If there is a week left in the sprint and not much to be completed, then sure, they might be able to power through. But what if the sprint just got started?

This leads us to the second school of thought: the cancellation of the sprint. In many ways, canceling a sprint that's in trouble right at the beginning is like asking an airplane to turn around and land shortly after takeoff. After all, why would you risk the airplane getting into trouble mid-flight when you could have addressed the issue as soon as it arose. In fact, it might be best to cancel the sprint, push it back a week and then start over, as opposed to admitting that things aren't going to work out two or three weeks into the sprint.

The fact of the matter is that it is important for the Scrum Master and the Product Owner to realize when things aren't going well and pulling the plug if it comes to that. Naturally, canceling a sprint will lead to delays and cost overruns, but at the end of the day, it is better to fall back slightly than to deliver poor quality products that may lead the customer to reject the product potentially causing the sprint to be lost altogether.

At this point, we can see that running a sprint can be both straightforward and challenging. It is always best for the Scrum Master and Product Owner to have contingency plans in place. That way, if any of the worst-case scenarios should ever take place, the team can be ready to deal with them. Otherwise, the cost of being unprepared may lead to disastrous results.

Chapter 10

SCALING SCRUM

One of the biggest criticisms of Scrum is that it is not suited for large-scale projects in which a great deal of people needs to intervene. After all, the recipe for Scrum calls for teams from four to 10 members. On paper, that is not conducive to effective projects in which there is a need for a large staff of people working together. In this chapter, we will look at what is known as the "Scrum of Scrums" and how it can be used to address this issue.

In short, Scrum can be scaled up to include a large number of teams working in unison. This large number of teams must all work on individual portions of the project that, when put together, they all add up to the big picture of the project.

Let's consider an example in order to bring this idea into focus.

A vehicle manufacturer is looking to build a new model for its upcoming sales season. Naturally, designing, building, testing, and eventually launching a new vehicle for production is no easy task. In fact, it requires a great deal of highly skilled people working together to produce a working prototype that can be presented to the public and eventually mass-produced.

So, the manufacturer has decided to adopt the Scrum methodology in order to build this new vehicle as it is eager to get it out as quickly as possible.

To do this, the project sponsor has identified the need for five teams:

- The design team
- The mechanical team

- The electrical team
- The body team
- The paint team

Each of these teams has a specific job they need to do in the construction of the vehicle.

For starters, the design team is in charge of coming up with the concept of the car. Is it going to be a sedan? Is it going to be an SUV? Is it going to be a truck?

That decision will depend on one thing: the User Stories that are created for the project.

Next, the mechanical team will figure out all of the mechanical components of the car, such as the engine, transmission, brakes, and so on. The electrical team will devise the electronics that will go into the care while the body team will actually sculpt the vehicle. Finally, the paint team will give the car its final touches and present it to the public.

All of these teams must all work in sync so that when the time comes for the car to be taken public, every-thing is ready by the deadline and within budget.

Now, a traditional approach would assemble each team one by one and only bring them on until one team has finished their part. What this means is that one team will sit by waiting for the previous team to get their part done. Then, when that team is done, there is nothing left for them to do.

In Scrum, all five teams are working together to figure out what they can do while the other teams are work-ing on their respective parts. All of this happens are the same time.

In order for this project to begin taking shape, the pro-ject sponsor must make one of the most crucial deci-sions of the entire project: the selection of the Project Product Owner. The Project Product Owner is the single point of responsibility that will come between the entire project team and the stakeholders. Bear in mind that the Project Product Owner is not the "boss" by any means. They have the same job as a regular Product Owner, except that they will be dealing with multiple Scrum Masters and as opposed to just the one team.

At this point, the Project Product Owner must develop the User Stories that will be included in the project. Whether there is just one story or multiple stories, is largely dependent on what the project sponsor and stakeholders decide they want.

Once the User Stories have been crafted, the Project Product Owner can then go about to look for the Scrum Masters that will be needed for this project. Each Scrum Master will be in charge of one team. Since our example is based on five teams, there will be five Scrum Masters. Each Scrum Master will carry out the functions of the Scrum Master as has been described thus far.

However, given the scope of this project, there is a sixth Scrum Master known as the Project Scrum Master. The Project Scrum Master is the Scrum Master of Scrum Masters. This particular role is in charge of collecting any and all information from the Scrum Masters in order to determine if there are individual issues that need to be addressed within a single team, or if there are issues affecting all teams.

Also, the Project Scrum Master may serve in a mentorship role providing guidance to the entire project team pertaining to the ways of Scrum, or even technical support if need be. The Project Scrum Master will hold a Daily Standup Meeting with the all of the Scrum Masters. The individual Scrum Masters, in turn, will hold their own Daily Standup Meeting. The information gathered from the individual Daily Standup Meetings will be then transmitted into the Daily Standup Meeting among all Scrum Masters.

The Project Scrum Master will be in constant communication with both the Project Product Owner and the individual Scrum Masters in order to ensure consistent communication throughout the project. All large-scale issues may be addressed at the Scrum Master level or taken up with the Project Product Owner.

Also, the Project Product Owner may keep tabs on individual Scrum Masters, but only if the situation somehow warrants the Project Product Owner's direct attention. In addition, the Project Scrum Master may keep tabs on individual developers if there is a situation that needs closer attention, such as a health problem or some piece of sensitive equipment that needs great care.

Another common concern about scaling Scrum is having multiple teams working at the same time. To this concern, it is important to note that all teams must be working on the same sprint at the same time. This means that all teams begin on the same date and end on the same date. Then, the aggregate product is put together for the customer to see.

In the example of the new vehicle, the customer might be able to see a finished sketch for the car's design, a glimpse of what interiors may look like, a prototype engine, a peek at the electronics included in the car, and color options.

All of these advances will allow the customer to see what they can expect from the final version of the vehicle once built. This showing will also allow the customer to raise any questions about colors, electronics, or anything else that they feel is relevant before it is actually put into the car. This opens the door for change requests that the customer may have about the vehicle.

Also, by having all teams work at the same time, it allows the team to build brand-new components that might be included in this model as part of innovations or upgrades over existing models. This is a key element to take into consideration as the team may be more willing to experiment with the components in the car as a means of building components that might no have been included otherwise.

One other important advantage of having all teams simultaneously working together saves time. So, instead of having teams wait until one team is done, they can all work together in order to achieve their own outcomes. Since the teams are not working in isolation, they can easily communicate and determine what they can do on their end.

For instance, the team working on the engine might be unsure about what dimensions to include for the engine since they don't know what the engine bay will look like on the car. This is a question that might come up at a Daily Standup Meeting. So, the Scrum Master of the mechanical team can sit down with the Scrum Master of the design and body team to decide what dimensions the engine bay will have. That way, both the body team and the mechanical team can work on their own designs.

As you can see, the means of communication are wide open in a project such as this. The difference is that instead of having all team members get together to hold large and unproductive meetings, they will centralize their communication through the Scrum Master. That way, questions can be addressed effectively, and time is not wasted. On the contrary, everyone has a chance to act accordingly and make the most of their current situation.

As with anything, there are complications that come up. Since a Scrum of Scrums implies a much larger project, the issues of a regular Scrum can become magnified. So, here are some ways in which these issues can be dealt with effectively in this context.

First of all, what happens when one team falls behind schedule, but everyone else is running on time?

This can become a serious issue if not addressed in time. When one of the teams happens to fall behind without clearly identifying the cause, the entire project might be put a risk for delays and cost overruns. That is why it is important for the Scrum Master to escalate any issues they feel might get out of hand. This will allow the entire project team to rally and figure out the best way to help individual teams address any potential issues.

Please bear in mind that Scrum is highly time-sensitive. So, being able to catch issues before they become a problem is essential to keeping large projects running smoothly and on time.

The next issue that large projects have to deal with is the loss of team members.

This is a very tricky issue. If a project has multiple members that are highly skilled and tough to replace, the Project Product Owner needs to ensure that everything is done to avoid these people from leaving without notice or there not being any suitable replacements.

However, if a project has multiple members who are easier to replace, then the team can make arrangements to have replacements lined up. For instance, our new vehicle project might make use of mechanics who don't have any specific expertise. Therefore, they can be replaced much more easily than a mechanic with a complex skillset such as assembling engines.

Nevertheless, a sudden loss of a large number of members might motivate the team to shut down the sprint and retool before moving forward. This is an extreme case, indeed, but it is worth keeping in mind. Often, it is best to shut down a sprint during a Scrum of Scrums because it is much harder to replace a large number of members than it would be to replace one or two highly skilled individuals.

Another important aspect to consider during a Scrum of Scrums is the risk of unforeseen, or even freak, circumstances.

As mentioned earlier, the Project Product Owner needs to be ready for anything that might possibly happen. Issues with the weather, electrical supply, available parts, or even a workers' strike might cause the project team to fall behind significantly.

The last thing that any Project Product Owner wants to do is cancel a sprint. This should be seen as a last resort and forced upon only be extenuating circumstances. Under duress, the Project Product Owner may consider it to be best to shut things down until the issue can be resolved. Naturally, canceling a sprint is a decision that must be made in conjunction with the customer. Furthermore, the project sponsor also needs to be on board, given the nature of the decision.

Yet, one question that is often avoided in most discussions regarding Scrum is about the possibility of canceling a project altogether. While killing a project altogether is the worst thing that could possibly happen, regardless of the project management methodology used, the fact of the matter is that such a situation could potentially happen.

The biggest reason why a project could be canceled altogether is when the customer runs out of money. In such cases, the customer needs to make sure that the project team is aware of what's happening so that progress is not lost entirely. After all, it could be a different product that could be completed, but without all of the functionalities that the customer had originally intended. The cancellation, or at least suspension, of a project, is greater when the scale is larger, and the cost is higher.

Also, the loss of a project sponsor might lead the customer to question the viability of a project. In that regard, the customer might not be entirely convinced of the project's effectiveness or feasibility once the project sponsor has been removed.

This is an important consideration as there are instances in which there is a wealthy benefactor or investor who is behind a project. But when, for one reason or another, the sponsor withdraws their support from the project (most likely financing), the entire project falls through the cracks. This opens the door to legal concerns over the property of the products developed up that point. That is why any Product Owner ought to make sure that these situations are provided for in the Project Charter and/or contracts that are signed at the outset of the project.

The last, perhaps most concerning issue within a Scrum or Scrums, is quality assurance.

Quality assurance is an issue regardless of the size and scope of the project. However, it becomes magnified when the project is large. In such cases, the Project Product Owner needs to make sure that they have made provisions to ensure that the quality of the outputs complies with the customer's acceptance criteria. Otherwise, having an output fail in a Scrum or Scrums may lead some teams' work to be considered complete while others may have to go back to the drawing board. This will cause the project to fall behind.

As such, quality assurance needs to be conducted within individual teams and then collectively once the sum of all components is put together.

In the example of a new vehicle design, each team needs to ensure that their part of the project is up to speed as per the customer's acceptance criteria, but when the time comes to build the entire vehicle, that is, put all of the individual parts together, the team needs to make sure that everything is working as it should.

In order to make sure that everything is working well in unison, a specific sprint can be convened in which all teams work in tandem to bring the car into a single piece. So, individual teams can carry out their own testing to make sure that the car is running properly.

Then, there needs to be one final phase in the sprint in which the entire team tests the vehicle. This could come in the form of a test drive. Once the working prototype has been cleared and the team deems it to comply with the customer's acceptance criteria, the final Sprint Review Meeting can be called in order for the customer to see the finished product.

In this example, let's assume that the final Sprint Review Meeting is held at the proving grounds in which a test driver conducts a test drive. Things such as speed, braking, and electronics are demonstrated to the customer, so they can see the final product.

Then, assuming the customer gives the green light to the product, the project comes to an end. At this point, the Scrum of Scrums is officially disbanded, and the Project Product Owner, along with the Project

Scrum Master, can begin the handover process of all relevant documentation, working components, and the final product itself.

In fact, in a project such as this one, individual team members may coach and train factory floor workers on how to assemble the vehicle and test the various components. While this would not be an official part of the project, it is certainly part of a larger scope of the customer's objectives.

As you can see, Scrum can be scaled up to suit larger projects. The fact that Scrum isn't typically viewed as the type of project management methodology used in non-software projects is largely based on the fact that most project management professionals are skilled in the ways of traditional methodologies. In such cases, it can be tough to transition into a methodology such as Scrum Master. Nevertheless, the applications of Scrum are clearly evident.

At this point, it is certainly worth pointing out that it is your choice to implement Scrum in any of your projects. While it can definitely be applied to virtually any field, the fact of the matter is that you need to make an assessment of your team's understanding and experience with Scrum. If you find that your team needs to sharpen their skills in this project management methodology, then it would benefit your team to get some training and improve their skills.

At the end of the day, the most important thing to keep in mind is that Scrum is just a means of achieving the ultimate goal, that is, achieving your project's objectives. So, it is important to translate your vision, or that of your customers, into language that your entire project team can clearly identify with. That alone is a single biggest step you can take to ensuring that your project will achieve its outcomes and meet the expectations of your customer.

So, do take the time to sit down and make sure those User Stories reflect the end-users who will benefit from your work. Putting a name and a face to these folks will help you get to the promised land and save a great deal of time, money, and effort.

CONCLUSION

We have come to the end of this book. But that doesn't mean we have to the end of this discussion. In fact, there is still plenty more to discuss. Scrum is still an evolving entity. That means that there is always something new being developed, something new being implemented, and something new being discovered.

The fact is that Scrum is the type of discipline that requires practitioners to be on a constant learning path. What that means is that you can find ways of making things work in your own field while learning about the success, and failures, others have had.

Moreover, your lack of success in one area is hardly a waste. Quite the opposite, it is a learning experience that you can use to your benefit. In that regard, things that don't go well are a way of ensuring meaningful learning experiences. These learning experiences then become lessons learned.

Consequently, all lessons learned which you can add to your knowledge base will only serve to increase your abilities in project management. Since Scrum is an evolving discipline, you have the opportunity to contribute to its evolution with your own experience and skills. This means that you can make a meaningful contribution to Scrum as a whole and to the specific field you have implemented it in.

If you are brand new to Scrum, don't worry; you will have a chance to contribute in a meaningful way as well. But it is important to bear in mind that making the most of these learning opportunities will serve as the basis for your own experience and doctrine.

So, what's next?

The next step is rather straightforward. Take what you have learned from this book and put it into practice in your own line of work.

If you are an experienced practitioner, there are surely aspects of this book that you can implement or even adapt to your own needs. You can certainly find ways of making the information contained in this book work to your own particular advantage.

In addition, you can use the concepts described in this book and contrast them with your own practices. This is the type of exercise that will surely help you gain a deeper understanding of your own project management style. This will go a long way toward helping you evolve your specific management style.

If you are a newbie to Scrum, then you have everything you need to get started. Perhaps this book will help you to lay the foundation for the arguments in favor of implementing Scrum in your organization. It will hopefully give you the ammunition you need to field any objections that might come your way. Often, it is the objections which you need to address far more than actual question pertaining to the feasibility of Scrum.

Ultimately, the choice of implementing Scrum is worth your while. Implementing Scrum may require your team to get some training while taking time out from their own schedules in order to get up to speed. But the fact of the matter is that Scrum is an investment that you can make in yourself and your team's capabilities.

So, what are you waiting for?

Do take the time to go over any part of this book that you feel you need to dig deeper into. Naturally, there are some parts that are easier for you to grasp than others. Some parts are easy to understand but challenging to put into practice. So, please keep in mind that practice with Scrum, not just as a means of project management but as a philosophy in the workplace, takes time to master, but it certainly pays off in the long run.

Finally, thank you for taking the time to read this book. If you have found it to be useful and informative, then, by all means, but what you have learned in this book into practice. You can use it as a basis for training others on your team and in your organization on the ways of Scrum. The information contained herein will help you to develop a training program that you can use to disseminate the ways of Scrum in an effective and easily digestible manner.

There are many other books on this subject available in the marketplace. As such, it can be hard to pick the right one. So, do your friends and favor and recommend this one. It is a great place to start for anyone who is new to Scrum or is looking to brush up on their skills.

Thank you once again. See you next time.